OCA 1967–1972
Five Turbulent Years

by Morris Wolfe

OCA 1967–1972
Five Turbulent Years

by Morris Wolfe

grub street books
TORONTO

ISBN 0-9689737-0-1

National Library of Canada Cataloguing in Publication

Wolfe, Morris
OCA 1967-1972 : five turbulent years / Morris Wolfe.

ISBN 0-9689737-0-1

1. Ontario College of Art--History. 2. Ascott, Roy. 3. Ontario College of Art--Presidents. I. Title.

N346.5.C32T67 2002 707.1'1713541 C2002-901294-5

The Macpherson cartoon on page 29 is reprinted with permission from The Toronto Star Syndicate. The photos and text on pages 22 and 60 are reprinted with permission from the Globe and Mail. Every effort has been made to trace copyright holders, and we apologize in advance for any unintentional omissions. We would be pleased to insert the appropriate acknowledgement in any subsequent edition of this publication.

PUBLISHED BY
grub street books, 1 Humbercrest Boulevard
Toronto, Ontario M6S 4K6

PRINTED IN CANADA, AND BOUND BY
Coach House Press

BOOK AND COVER DESIGN
Ben Wolfe Design (bwolfe@mac.com)

for Menya,
who would have loved
this wonderful crazy place

Contents

Acknowledgements

THIS PROJECT BEGAN with two archival exhibits in the spring of 2000 dealing with the history of OCAD. I'm grateful to a number of people, without whose help those exhibits would not have taken place. Laura Griffiths, with the assistance of Teresa Zywulko, organized the OCAD Archives. Joyce Young catalogued the College's Permanent Collection and curated *Hidden Treasures*, an exhibit of work from the Collection. Laura, Teresa and Joyce, third year students at the time, then assisted me in mounting *rewind/pause/play*, an exhibit in the OCAD Gallery of material from the Archives and Permanent Collection. The exhibits were to celebrate the College's 125th anniversary.

Seka Sefter of the Development Office and Christine Swiderski and her able staff at the OCAD Gallery assisted with numerous details. An anonymous donor, Julian Bowron and the late Morris Granatstein generously donated money to pay the students who worked on the project. Ron Shuebrook, Vice-President Academic, granted me two half periods of release time from teaching during the 1999-2000 academic year to work in the Archives. Without the unstinting support of Cindy Ball, Director of Development, and Jill Patrick, Director of Library Services, none of the above could have taken place.

A number of people read and commented on various drafts of *OCA 1967–1972: Five Turbulent Years*: Barbara Astman, Matt Behan, Ian Carr-Harris, Gary Michael Dault, Nancy Dillow, Rosemary Donegan, Archie Graham, Robert Hedrick, Dennis Reid, Richard Rhodes, Keith Rushton, Jim Tiley, Diana Vazquez, Michèle White, Jennifer Wolfe, and Paul Young. I'm grateful to all of them. They, of course, are not to blame for the contents;

errors of fact or judgement are mine alone. My son, Ben Wolfe, edited and designed this little book, which I completed during a sabbatical.

More than anyone, I want to thank Joy Cohnstaedt, my partner in life, who makes everything easier.

Preface

THE ONE THING almost everyone connected with the Ontario College of Art & Design knows about the history of the place is that a man named Ascott became President at some point in the past, that he was fired, and that everything that's gone wrong at the College since then is his fault. A competing version of the story has it that Ascott was actually the Messiah and that everything that's gone wrong since his time at the College is the result of his crucifixion. This small book examines the turbulent events that led to Ascott's hiring and the even more turbulent events that occurred during his very brief — ten month — tenure as President.

I began teaching at OCA, as it was then called, on September 1, 1971, having been hired by its new President, Roy Ascott. I took early retirement from the College on September 1, 2001. In June 1972, at the end of my first year at the College, I published an article entitled "Ascott in Wonderland," in *Toronto Life*. When I wrote the piece, I didn't know enough about the College's history, particularly the events that had led to Ascott's hiring. OCAD's newly organized Archives have enabled me to do now what I couldn't do then.

Morris Wolfe
September 2001
morris@morriswolfe.com

Chapter One
BACKGROUND

In 1960 bells rang to indicate the beginning and end of classes at the Ontario College of Art. Nude male models wore jock straps. Students and faculty had little or no say in the running of the College. OCA's sleepy governing body, Council, met twice a year to rubber stamp decisions made by the Principal, Sydney Watson. In a 1962 interview, Watson was asked if there were a lot of rebels at OCA. "No," he replied, a "student can't rebel or he isn't going to graduate." Is that a good thing, he was asked. "It's good for us," said Watson. "It makes it a lot easier … to run the College." In its various incarnations, OCA had been run that way since its founding in 1876.

In the mid-60s, the aims and purposes of education were being hotly debated; alternative schools were springing up everywhere. Many of us believed that radical change was possible. Throughout North America, students were demanding a greater say in the running of postsecondary institutions. The nature of the curriculum — and who controlled it — was central to their concerns. Faculty wanted a greater say, too. In the fall of 1965, four OCA teachers — drawing and painting instructors John Alfsen, Aba Bayefsky, Alan Collier and Eric Freifeld — announced that they were organizing a faculty association. Sydney Watson was furious. How dare they do such a thing without asking him first.

When the faculty scheduled an organizational meeting for October 15, Watson called a faculty meeting of his own on the 14th. He told the teachers they'd never had it so good. Bayefsky warned Watson that if he discouraged the faculty from attending the meeting on the 15th, he could make it embarrassing for the College by going to the media. Twenty-seven of the 30 faculty who attended the organizational meeting voted to establish OCAFA (the Ontario College of Art Faculty Association). Bayefsky was elected president and a committee was struck to prepare a constitution. One of the three faculty who voted no was Bill Poole, a design teacher. He suspected the motives of the organizers.

Alfsen, Bayefsky, Collier and Freifeld did in fact have other motives in founding OCAFA. The four men were figurative artists, all members of the Drawing and Painting department (D&P). Their approach to teaching was academic and conservative and that's how they wanted things to remain. They were convinced that life drawing should be at the centre of *all* art and design education. In recent years they'd seen course offerings in other areas of the College expanding, especially in design. More students were now graduating from the College in the applied arts than in fine arts. The figurative artists had persuaded themselves that they were being phased out and that Watson planned to turn OCA into a design school. Freifeld, the leading figure among the old guard, has been described by former students and colleagues as mercurial, as an articulate and Machiavellian politician, and as an autocratic but delightful raconteur and performer in the classroom. Bayefsky was more robust, more openly ambitious. He became the principal spokesman for the conservative forces in D&P.

The figurative artists saw enemies outside the College, too. The Toronto art scene had become dominated by abstraction during the previous half dozen years. The figurative artists were convinced that abstraction was an enormous fraud, a fad that would soon pass. In speeches and articles, they lashed out at the enemy. In a 1963 talk, for example, Alan Collier complained that the abstractionists couldn't draw and were getting by on gimmicks: "Everyone is slathering paint, using big black lines that kick the viewer in the stomach.... The real rebel today is the man who paints a tree to look like a tree." (According to Graham Coughtry, "Every damn tree in the country has been painted.") The abstractionists, who had earlier responded with vitriol of their own, had now begun sounding almost conciliatory. "I am not against figurative painting," said William Ronald, an artist not known for his temperate views. "As long as a painting is good, whether it's non-objective or realist, it is worthwhile. I would certainly turn to figurative painting if I thought I could express myself better through it. Eight years ago," he added, "I wouldn't have said that … you mustn't set rules … either for yourself or for others."

Watson, too, saw enemies outside OCA. Critics of the College were becoming increasingly vocal. In an essay in the fall 1965 issue of *Canadian Art*, May Cutler, a Montreal publisher and critic, said the College was twenty years behind the times in its approach to teaching fine art. "[OCA] is probably as traditional, academic, self-satisfied and … removed from the mainstreams of modern art as any school in North America. Since the death of the great painter-teacher Jock Macdonald [in 1960], OCA has contributed almost nothing by way of serious artists to the country." In a column in the *Toronto Telegram*, Mashel Teitelbaum, painter and iconoclast, mocked OCA's announcement that it had turned away 1,000 students that September. "The College did them a favour," he wrote. "The .05 per cent of this contingent with talent will [do] better on their own…. Not a day passes at such places as [OCA] that the truth does not twig in the dim subconscious of the least imaginative student or teacher: What in the hell has this to do with art? With life? What in hell am I doing here?"

Watson wasn't accustomed to public scrutiny. Almost every time he spoke to the media, he put his foot in his mouth. A year earlier, for example, he'd been drawn into the debate about what Canada's new flag should look like. When asked what he thought of the winning entry — i.e. the flag we now fly — he said that "if a student … submitted this design with his application to enter the college, he would not be admitted." End of discussion. Watson's initial response to Cutler was that the creation of artists wasn't "a primary concern of the school." He quoted the section of the OCA Act that defined the College's purpose as "the training of students in the fine arts, including, drawing, painting, designing, modelling and sculpture, and in all branches of the applied arts in the more artistic trades and manufactures." Cutler argued that the *first* part of that definition — the focus on the fine arts — ought to be the primary goal of OCA. All the major British and North American art colleges that combine fine and applied art instruction, she said, "recognize that their fine arts courses are the core, against which all other courses are judged."

In a letter to the editor, Aba Bayefsky offered his own take on May

A New Idea: Art In Art Schools

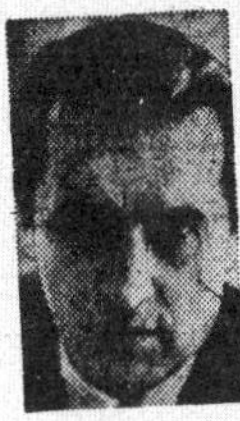

DISSENT

by MASHEL TEITELBAUM

THE Ontario College of Art has turned away 1,000 students applying for September enrolment. In a negative way the College did them a favor. The .05 per cent. of this contingent with talent will make out better on their own; the others can provide the necessary social background in some other setting.

Not a day passes at such places as the Ontario College of Art or other provincial art schools but that the truth doesn't twig in the dim subconscious of the least imaginative student or teacher: What in hell has this to do with art? With life? What in hell am I doing here?

The present hang-up in art education can be traced to the institutionalization of the old master's studio, and the straight-jacketing of the creative process into the grade-school system. Following a 200-year span, and rapidly accelerating obsolescence since the turn of the century, this type of school — except for technical-training purposes — is now ready for the scrap-heap.

Instead of adding to these outmoded beehives of mediocrity, the powers-that-be should consider encouraging a new type of art school at the university level. A dozen of the new universities have a start-from-scratch opportunity to setup art schools with some relevance to this fast-changing world.

Although, this being Canada, nothing is likely to be done in this vital area, for the record, I'd like to blueprint a possible art school of the future.

Organization would be based on a separation of the administrative and teaching functions. The administrative staff would be permanent; the teaching staff would rotate yearly. This would free each to do the best in each area without undue cross-interference.

The teaching freedom afforded, plus the one-year tenure, would make the teaching role attractive to top professionals in a way that hasn't been possible in this country in the past. Also this would minimize the usual problems of staff politics, dead woodism or on-the-job superannuation which afflicts present art schools. The advantages to the student and teacher would be complimentary and multiple.

This school would set up a creative environment in which the learning-teaching process could happen: where the student would have the freedom and constant challenge to test his notions, ideas, feelings and abilities . . . and the teacher would have the academic freedom to encourage this activity without fear or favor.

I like to think of this school as the "Socratic-shop school." It would consist of a free arrangement of glassed studio-classrooms around a central administrative core, containing offices, library, student and teacher lounges, cafeterias, store-rooms and stores.

In this spacious, informal and relaxed atmosphere, the student would be free to shop the Socratic-shops (the teacher-dominated studios) to find, each for himself, a meaningful challenge, medium and mentor.

This program would dispense with all impediments to the learning-teaching process — grades, credits, attendance records, etc. — and concentrate attention on individual development and creative effort.

It seems to me that in a climate favorable to increased spending for the arts, before we proceed to add to existing obsolete institutions — to encourage the random proliferation of half-baked, hayseed arts projects — we should pause briefly and consider what, if anything, is being accomplished.

However, it would be pie-in-the-sky to hold out any hope for this long-denied long-neglected educational area.

This is a bleak picture for young art aspirants to face. But should they begin to understand the why of this, the closer they will come to the basis and source of meaningful art activity in this time . . . given the low hand Canadian society deals them.

Mr. Teitelbaum, a Toronto artist, is former professor of art at the University of Manitoba.

Toronto Telegram, September 3, 1965

Cutler. "… what seems to infuriate [the College's] critics," he said, "is that [OCA] has a staff of accomplished, dedicated and sensitive artists. [A] large segment of the world of art, with its commercial orientation, its concern for novelty and its fascination with itself, has become increasingly isolated and resentful; … in the educational system they perceive a powerful challenge to their outlook…."

II

COUNCIL HAD APPOINTED Sydney Watson Principal in 1955, replacing L.A.C. Panton, who had died. Principals at OCA had no fixed terms; they served until age 65 or until they died, whichever came first. (J.E.H. Macdonald had also died in office in 1932.) Watson, with his greying crew-cut and thick black framed glasses, looked like a high school principal. He lived in Rosedale, which would have pleased members of Council, was largely self-taught as a designer and artist, best known for his murals and his expertise in typography. He too was suspicious of abstraction, but for a different reason. Far too many Jews had been involved in its origins, he told one young painting teacher.

Watson may not have been savvy in his dealings with the media, but he was government savvy, effective at extracting funds for the expansion of OCA. In the years following World War Two, governments began throwing money at postsecondary education and did so, it now seems, with as little forethought as they've displayed in cutting back on postsecondary funding in more recent years. In the late 1940s, the money enabled war veterans to get a postsecondary education, society's way of thanking them for their service. In the 1950s, governments decided that the 'new economy' required a better trained workforce. More money was found. When the Russian satellite, Sputnik, was launched in October 1957, still more money became available, including money from the federal government. If we were going to help beat the Russkies, we had to produce more scientists and technicians. New universities sprang up almost overnight; a community college system was created. Many of those institutions established visual arts programs of their own.

One of the beneficiaries of government largesse was OCA. Watson came up with a rationale for expanding the College, and money came his way. He argued, for instance, that if Ontario was to keep pace with the U.S. in product design, an Industrial Design department was needed. (Not a bad idea.) In 1957, a first addition to OCA's original 1922 building in Grange Park was opened. Watson hired American industrial designers, trained in Bauhaus techniques. The College could now accommodate 450 full-time students, up from 320 in 1952. But Watson made it clear that when he approached governments for money, he talked design. "They would never give this money to a strictly 'long hair' ... art institution," he said, and then, as a kind of afterthought, commented, "but we still think of OCA as an art school.... There has never been a change in policy; this has just grown. This new wing will allow ... us to cut down on the size of classes and relieve the pressure." Five years later, in September 1962, a second addition was built, paid for by the Ontario government, with assistance from the federal department of labour.

The decision to grow the College was taking place in the absence of long range planning or debate. If a plan existed, it existed solely in the mind of Sydney Watson and was then given the imprimatur of Council. I can find no record in the OCAD Archives or elsewhere of a discussion by Council about whether the College should expand, and if so, by how much, and in what areas. Growth, in and of itself, was assumed to be A Good Thing. It's not surprising that the expansion of the design side of the College was helping feed the paranoia of the figurative artists. OCAFA, they believed, would give faculty a seat at the table when such decisions were made.

III

In the fall of 1965, two of Toronto's leading abstractionists — Dennis Burton and Robert Hedrick — established The New School of Art as an alternative to what they saw as the stultifying atmosphere in fine art at OCA. The New School had no entrance or attendance requirements, no grades, no marks, and no diploma. Its faculty believed that too much time was spent in traditional schools on paperwork. "If people want to learn, they will learn," said John Sime, the school's administrator. "I don't believe in competition with anyone but yourself. If you need the clutch of a diploma, there are plenty of places you can go to get one." The only thing that really counted, he said, was the quality of one's portfolio.

Among the New School's instructors were Graham Coughtry, Arthur Handy, Ross Mendes, Gordon Rayner, Robert Markle, and Paul Young, each of whom was free to teach what and how they wanted. "Most of my instructors," said Sime, "get paid less than house painters on an hourly basis but 80 per cent of them had their own shows in major galleries last year … that is not true of OCA instructors." The New School was in financial difficulty from the beginning. The city of Toronto, for instance, insisted that it install a $2000 fire alarm system; all schools had to do so. The federal government, on the other hand, said the New School wasn't a school, and denied it the tax deduction that might have allowed it to pay for an alarm system. In those days, OCA was receiving about $300,000 a year from the province and the New School about $25,000 from the Canada Council and the Ontario Arts Council.

Chapter Two
1967–1968

In September 1967 another addition to OCA was scheduled to open, the third in ten years. This addition, containing new shops for sculpture, ceramics and textiles, would make OCA the largest college of art and design in North America, a fact that Sydney Watson noted with pride. In January 1967, eight months before the new wing was to come into use, Watson informed Council that he was changing the curriculum. He was going to amalgamate the previously independent departments of drawing and painting, sculpture, and material arts into a Fine Art Department. "[T]he wider areas of expression now demanded of sculptors, painters and craftsmen," he wrote, "makes such a change … not only practical but desirable." Students would now have more choice than they'd had previously. Following Foundation Year, Fine Art students would take a common second year, divided equally among painting, sculpture and crafts. In third year, they would declare a major and a minor. In fourth year, as much as two-thirds of a student's studio time could be devoted to the major — drawing and painting, say. But that meant less time than they now had, less control of the curriculum than the figurative painters in D&P had now.

As usual, there had been little or no consultation by Watson in drawing up his plan. When he announced the changes to a student assembly, including the requirement that all students take shops, five women students, who had come to OCA specifically to study drawing and painting, heckled him. Other students and faculty were furious. Neither OCAFA nor the Students' Administrative Council (SAC) had been consulted. On Friday

March 31, students at the College held a sit-in, demanding that the shops be made elective and that Watson meet with them the following Monday to discuss the issue. The sit-in made the news. The April 1, 1967 issue of the *Globe* reported that 600 students had staged a 35 minute "sit-down" in the OCA auditorium. An accompanying photograph showed students carrying signs that read: "20 Years Behind? Was May Cutler Right?" and "At OCA they let us pay but never say."

Students complained that they already had little or no freedom in choosing their courses. Now they were being offered 'compulsory' choices. Keith Hillmer, a third-year advertising student and the President of SAC, told the *Globe*, that there hadn't been a basic change in the curriculum at OCA in seventeen years. "The place is archaic," he said. "I worked in advertising for three years part-time and in the summer. There's a lack of awareness of this outside world at the College." Paul Sterback, a 23-year-old D&P student, spoke of the backwardness of the D&P program. "They don't recognize any change has occurred since 1900. They still believe in the Renaissance ideal. When students suggest modern experiments, they laugh."

The following Monday, April 3, the students gathered in the auditorium during their regular 10:30 a.m. break. Watson had promised he would speak to them if they were "quiet and well-behaved." They kept their side of the bargain, but Watson failed to appear. Normally, the auditorium was cleared by a guard at 11 a.m., when classes resumed. To protest Watson's no show, the students remained in the auditorium until 11:35 a.m. (OCA students had always been rather docile when it came to protests. Although the story may well be apocryphal, I'm told that during J.E.H. MacDonald's tenure as Principal, the students walked out, protesting some real or imagined slight, and congregated in Grange Park. At tea time, MacDonald came out with an offering of milk and cookies. The protest was over.)

Watson addressed a student assembly the following day, Tuesday. He'd been consulting with SAC and had come up with a revised proposal. A limited elective program would begin in the fall. Second year students would get one elective; third year students would have four; fourth year students could have up to five. (The course load at the time was 10 periods — morning and afternoon classes five days a week! Full-time faculty taught eight periods.) Fourth year students throughout the College could negotiate up to three unsupervised periods. Department heads would meet students monthly to work out wrinkles. Watson also endorsed the principle of a joint staff, student, faculty committee and announced he would spend the summer visiting art and design schools in the U.S. and abroad to study their administrative structures. When he finished speaking, the students cheered him. Watson was, of course, delighted, convinced that what he termed "the revolution and counter-revolution" were over. He was going to lead the movement to reform OCA. Hillmer and SAC were pleased too. The Principal had demonstrated that he *could* listen to reason. "[N]ext September," said Watson, "we shall have not only the largest College of its kind in North America but the finest and certainly the most progressive."

At its May meeting, Watson informed Council that the changes in curriculum he'd proposed had been accepted by students and faculty in all departments; D&P was now on side too. He noted "that with the exception of two or three instructors, the new program [has] been enthusiastically accepted by all Heads of Departments and instructional staff." He reported that he had established a 'partnership' with the University of Guelph, allowing OCA students to complete a Bachelor of Fine Art at Guelph, while completing their AOCA — their Associate of the Ontario College of Art Diploma. But that meant taking university courses every summer for four years. (OCA had been talking about degree granting status since 1924, when George A. Reid first raised the possibility.)

II

IN SEPTEMBER 1967, Aba Bayefsky presented Watson with a draft Memorandum of Agreement that had been prepared by OCAFA. Among other things, the document proposed the establishment of tenure — a guarantee of permanent employment for senior faculty. Watson knew what had motivated the OCAFA proposal and took his time replying, stating that at a recent meeting, Council had decided it "would take no action whatsoever in this matter at the present time, and that any staff member

Dropout rash – OCA

Paul Mandell, chairman of the Student's Administrative Council of the Ontario College of Art announced Tuesday he is quitting both SAC and OCA.

Mandell gives his reasons for resigning as disenchantment with the course. He said, "OCA is not a very good school, as it is overcrowded and under-equipped."

A third-year advertising student, Mandell is one of 36 students who have resigned this year. He said some of his reasons for quitting are: financial problems, quality of instruction and general dissatisfaction with the school.

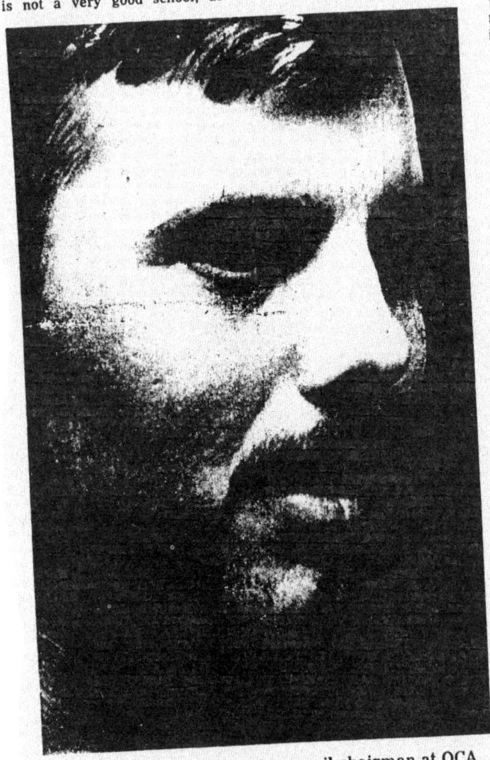

PAUL MANDEL, student's council chairman at OCA.

Principal of OCA, Sydney H. Watson, feels there is no general student dissatisfaction with the school. He said, "I am unaware of student unrest as nothing has been brought to my attention."

Mandell is the liaison between OCA and Ryerson in conjunction with Winter Carnival Week. He will not hand in his resignation until Carnival Week is over as he feels the carnival's success would be affected.

Fred Byfield, spokesman for Ryerson's Blue and Gold Society, said, "As long as Mandell stays behind the carnival, its success won't be affected, and anyway, plans are too far advanced to be hurt by his resignation."

This is not the first case of student unrest at OCA. Last March 700 students staged a one-hour sit-in to protest over the lack of choice in subjects. To pacify the students, a limited selective program was introduced in September of 1967.

Hippie pitches

Yorkville hippies will play ball with the law.

On one side of Yorkville Ave. last week, two hippies were playing handball when the law appeared on the other side of the street.

The hippies, noticing "the fuzz," passed the ball to one of the officers, who passed it back to the long-haired Villager.

After a few tosses, one of the officers remarked, "See, you play ball with us, and we'll play ball with you."

"Yeah," said the hippie, "we either lamport or lump it," referring to Controller Allan Lamport's constant criticism of Yorkville.

The Ryersonian, January 31, 1968

with suggestions or grievances should deal directly through the Principal." A more complete response would be presented at the February 5, 1968 meeting of Council.

But before then, *The Ryersonian*, a lively student paper published by journalism students at Ryerson Polytechnic, reported that Paul Mandell, the new chair of SAC, had announced he was quitting both SAC and the College. The reason for his decision became clear at the February 5 meeting. Watson reported that in early November he'd received a letter signed by all six chairs, proposing the establishment of a Board of Chairmen. He had immediately accepted their proposal, he said, and he and they had met weekly since then, including a weekend retreat at which "many constructive and stimulating ideas regarding curriculum, student welfare and management" were discussed. Watson went on to say that before Christmas, Paul Mandell had asked for SAC representation on Council. (The OCA Act didn't allow for that.) Watson told Mandell that instead he could attend the first Board of Chairmen meeting each month but he would have to submit the items he wanted discussed three days in advance — i.e. he wouldn't be coming to the table as an equal but as a supplicant. Mandell responded by leaving the College.

At the February 5 meeting, Council was deliberately mealy-mouthed on the subject of tenure. "It was felt," said the minutes, "that changing values and uncertainties ... in the contemporary art scene, although justifying a more generous practice of Sabbatical Leave [makes] the practicability of [instituting] tenure at this time questionable. The College would welcome from the Staff, however, any practical suggestions in this regard for consideration in the future." The figurative painters in D&P, those most concerned about the changes in curriculum and the establishment of tenure, were feeling vulnerable. They needed to make something happen.

Two weeks later, 200 students gathered in the auditorium to cheer John Bowman, the leader of a group of angry D&P students. They were protesting the rumour that Watson was phasing out D&P and turning OCA into a design school. The students called on him to resign. One of them carried a placard, reading: "What are you afraid of, Mr. Watson, democracy?" When Watson appeared and attempted to speak, Bowman announced, "This meeting has been declared closed."

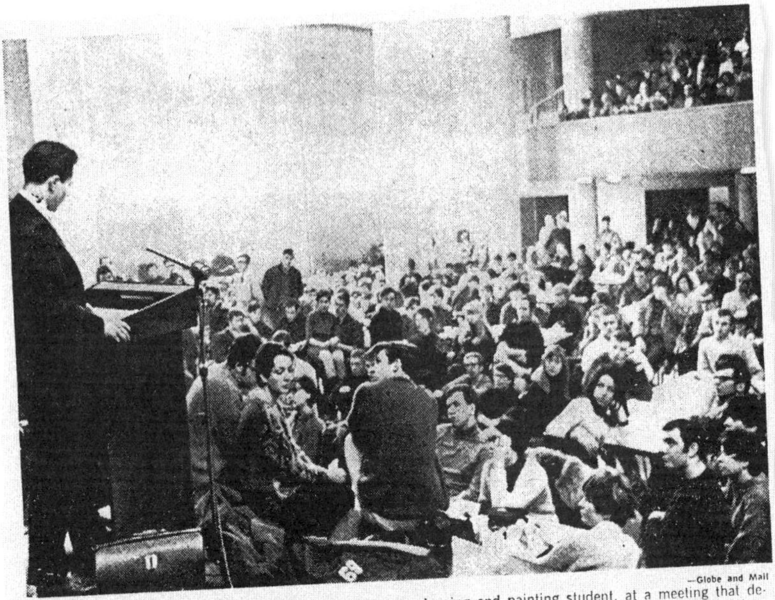

—Globe and Mail

Ontario College of Art students listen to John Bowman, a drawing and painting student, at a meeting that demanded a greater voice for students in the fine arts department. Principal was called a liar by a staff member.

Instructor charges principal lying in student power fight at OCA

The principal was called a liar by a member of his staff, the fine arts students of the Ontario College of Art demanded the principal's resignation, and the entire student body was badly split yesterday over the issue of student power.

Sitting in the middle of it all principal Sydney Watson didn't give an inch until the threat of a march on Queen's Park by the dissident students persuaded him to meet student and faculty representatives.

After the meeting, Mr. Watson said he would answer within a week student demands for a voice in the policy decisions of the fine arts department. Any changes, he said, would have to be submitted to the college's board of chairmen.

Mr. Watson agreed to recommend to the college's directors that student-staff consultative committees be set up in all departments of the college.

The stormy day began with a meeting between Mr. Watson and the fine arts students to discuss their charges that he was secretly changing the course and had ordered department chairman Carl Schaeffer not to discuss the matter with anyone. The students say Mr. Watson **is** attempting to weaken the course and perhaps eventually eliminate it. They asked for a democratic administration of the department.

When Mr. Watson denied he had sworn Mr. Schaeffer to secrecy he was accused of lying by painting and drawing instructor Aba Bayefsky. Mr. Bayefsky said "the principal did ask Mr. Schaeffer not to inform the faculty of any contemplated changes and we went to see Mr. Watson and he repeated the statement at that time."

"I've been called a liar by a member of my own staff. I appreciate that very much," Mr. Watson broke in.

Mr. Watson attempted to make a further statement but student chairman John Bowman told him the meeting was over.

Later, representatives of the 120 fine arts students attempted to get the majority of the 1,030 students at OCA to support their demand for Mr. Watson's resignation. It was a woolly session with the fine arts students forming a vocal left-wing minority, heckling the complacence, or caution, of students in the industrial design and commercial art departments.

The meeting began with Mr. Bowman reading a denunciation of dishonest dealing. The students groaned when they heard the florid wording, but cheered when told it was the preamble to the Magna Carta.

Mr. Bowman said the issue of student democracy was at the heart of the conflict. "Mr. Watson's hypocrisy in dealing with the painting and drawing department is in complete contradiction of the spirit of democracy.

"Deceitful is a mild word for it; he has lied . . . Do you want a liar for a principal?"

Shelley Shaw, a strawberry blond member of the committee of fine arts representatives, came forward to read out the demand for Mr. Watson's resignation, which was to be presented to Education Minister William Davis. The letter claimed the principal had denied students their constitutional rights by refusing to meet them despite three invitations last week.

Globe and Mail, February 20, 1968

Later that day, a second meeting was held, this one organized by the new chair of SAC, Wes D'Angelo, and attended by about 500 students. The meeting censured Bowman for not having allowed Watson to speak and for having done an end run around SAC; it was up to SAC to speak on behalf of the student body, he said. D&P students at the meeting said they'd heard that Watson had told their chair, Carl Schaefer, not to discuss changes that were about to be made with either students or faculty. Watson denied having said any such thing. Aba Bayefsky affirmed that he had. "I've been called a liar by a member of the staff," said Watson. "I appreciate that very much." Schaefer, who was at the meeting, remained silent.

Watson rejected the suggestion that an elected committee of D&P students and faculty be established to authorize changes in the curriculum. The College, he said, is "trying to get caught up with every other school on the continent. Any school which doesn't change its curriculum might as well fold up." May Cutler couldn't have put it better. The rebels, he said, consisted of a small group of conservative students who only wanted to study "old masters rather than contemporary art." (He didn't mention conservative faculty.) An angry Bowman responded, calling Watson an "intellectual thug." Eric Freifeld accused Watson of "incompetence." The one suggestion Watson agreed to was the establishment of a College-wide curriculum committee, comprised of students, faculty and administrators. But he'd made that promise before and nothing had been done. That's why Mandell had resigned.

At a meeting of the Board of Chairmen the next morning, Watson recommended that Bayefsky and Freifeld be fired and that disciplinary action be taken against Bowman. OCA's contract at the time stated that a faculty member could be immediately terminated without cause with the consent of the Minister of Education. The Board of Chairmen — including Schaefer — unanimously supported Watson's recommendation. Watson then sought, and was given, the approval of the Executive Committee of Council; after that he phoned Bill Davis, the Minister of Education, to advise him of the dismissals. Davis, unaware of what the OCA contract said, assured Watson that to his knowledge he had no jurisdiction in the matter.

On Wednesday February 21, Bayefsky and Freifeld received notes, summoning them to Watson's office. There they were met by Watson and the six department chairs (including Schaefer) and were handed letters, stating, "Your services as an instructor at this college are terminated immediately ... please remove all your personal possessions from the College building today." Bowman was also handed a letter. He was to stop slandering OCA at 'wildcat' meetings and to work for change through SAC — or be expelled. He also faced expulsion if he spoke to the media about what had taken place. Bowman promptly announced that he was quitting the College and told the media that Watson had tried to buy him with his diploma. "He waved [it] in my face like 30 pieces of silver.... I don't want to graduate from [that] kind of school...." What would have been the point, he said, of taking his concerns to SAC; Watson controlled SAC. (He seemed oblivious to the fact that he himself might be being manipulated.)

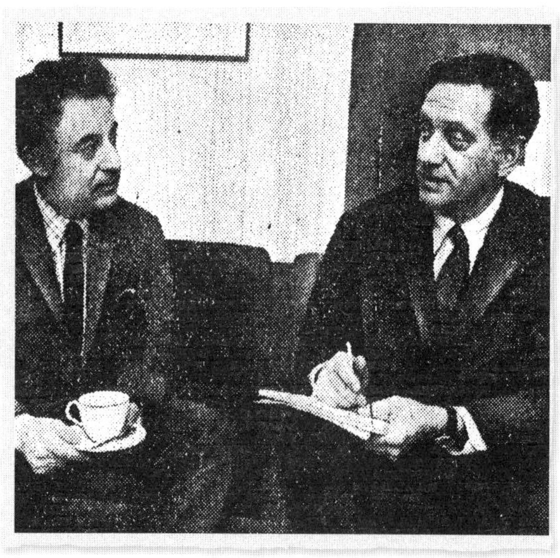

Eric Freifeld and Aba Bayefsky (Toronto Star photo)

Everyone entering the College the next morning was handed an announcement: "We wish to inform you that Mr. Aba Bayefsky and Mr. Eric Freifeld have been dismissed *effective immediately* from the staff of this College. John Bowman (IV D&P), Chairman of the Students' Committee, has been threatened with expulsion. By making such reprisals on individuals, the administration is obviously attempting to curtail the right to dissent and express opinion openly. ...we *must* express our disapproval of this outrageous action. We appeal to the entire student body and to the staff to join us in a protest in the main foyer at 9:30 this morning." Five hundred stu-

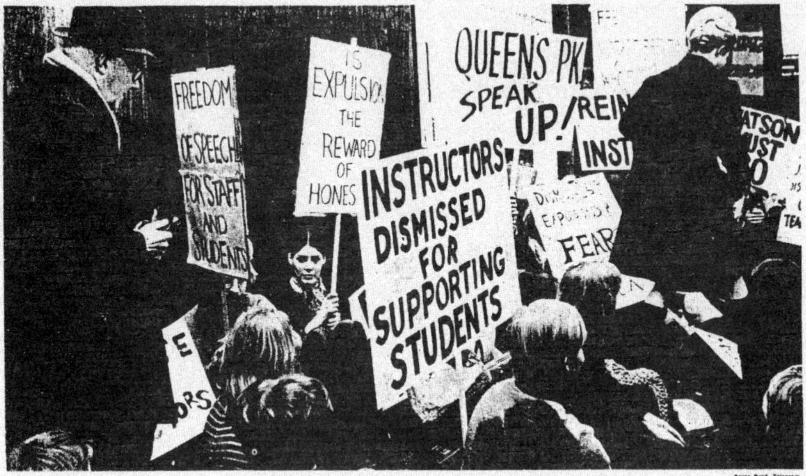

Bruce Reed, Telegram

Ontario College of Art principal Sydney H. Watson pushes through protesting students to get into the school. They are demanding Mr. Watson resign, and two fired teachers be reinstated.

PROTESTS ***600 angry art students back two fired teachers***

Toronto Telegram, February 22, 1968

dents boycotted classes and joined the protest. So did five D&P faculty members: John Newman, John Inglis, Tom LaPierre, John Alfsen and John Labonte-Smith.

Thirty-five other faculty members, including a number of members of OCAFA, issued a statement in defence of Watson:

> 1. We do not support the protests nor the manner in which they have been conducted. … the inciting of students … was a breach of contract leading to the almost total disruption of classes in several departments.
> 3. … we believe that due to [the] conduct [of the two faculty] … the Administration was left with no alternative but to dismiss them.
> 5. … the brief circulating among certain students and staff concerning the 'phasing out' of Drawing and Painting is based purely on an erroneous rumour….

Paul Young, who taught drawing to advertising and illustration students, was one of those who signed the statement. "There is not one member of the D&P faculty," he later wrote, "who has a pre-eminent or even eminent reputation as a Canadian artist. There is not one, young or old, who holds the slightest position in the contemporary art milieu, and make no mistake, that's where the young students are going to have to cut it and damn soon. … Faced with an entrenched and reactionary faculty … the [Principal] was probably correct to act unilaterally [to try to change things]. The irony is that the students thought *he* was the conservative…."

Watson distributed two statements of his own. The first went to faculty:

> It is expected that all instructors will during class hours give their undivided attention to the duties for which they are contracted. …
>
> 1. Any instructor has a democratic right to express his views regarding the Administration of the College, properly and through appropriate channels.
> 2. At the same time it is the duty of every member of staff to support the Administration's policy and teaching program until such times [sic] as changes are made.
> 3. It is completely antithetical to the duty of an instructor to indulge in public denunciation of the Principal and Administration of the College.
> 4. No further disciplinary action is contemplated at this time, and it is hoped that there will be no necessity for such action in the future."

The same memo was distributed to students, with two additional clauses:

> 5. Each Department Chairman is willing to meet democratically elected representatives of his Department to discuss matters of communication and policy. …
> 6. There are no existing consideration [sic] or plans to 'phase out', amalgamate or downgrade the Department of Drawing and Painting.

Schaefer met with the executive of SAC and informed them that he had been deliberately misrepresented by Bayefsky and Freifeld. But it was too late. On Wednesday February 28, 1200 full- and part-time OCA students marched to Queen's Park, waving signs and carrying a coffin, symbolizing the death of academic freedom at the College. Some of the signs read: "Watson's action demands reaction." "To be free is to create." And "Is this Toronto or Alabama?" The students were so orderly that Robert Nixon, leader of the Liberal opposition in Ontario, described their protest as "one of the freshest … since the farmers came up here on their tractors." Staff met a delegation of OCA students and briefed Davis, who then spent an hour with them. The students made three demands: that the fired teachers be reinstated; that a democratic restructuring of OCA take place; and that no action be taken against the protestors.

Davis was grooming himself to succeed John Robarts as premier and was, of course, eager to demonstrate his ability to deal quickly and effectively with thorny issues. He invited Watson, the chair of Council, and the vice-chair to his office. Public opinion, right or wrong, he told them, was going to take precedence. And the public's opinion was that Bayefsky and Freifeld had been fired for exercising their freedom of speech and that a student who had spoken out had been threatened with expulsion. Davis said he had agreed to meet OCA's student body the next day. He was going to announce that he was appointing Douglas Wright, a deputy minister, to review the administrative structure of the College, including the OCA Act. He also wanted to announce that Bayefsky and Freifeld were being reinstated. Watson balked at that. There must be some way, he said, that the administration's point of view could be put before the public. But Watson's ineptness with the media — and Bayefsky and Freifeld's media savvy — had already lost him that possibility. Davis said the only other possibility was a judicial inquiry into what had occurred and if that's what OCA wanted, he would make an announcement to that effect. The College had until the following morning to decide whether it wanted a judicial inquiry.

OCA's lawyer advised Watson, the chair, and vice-chair that such an inquiry could drag on, might well have negative political implications for the College, and would likely have little or no influence on public opinion. He suggested that the College ask Davis to extract a public apology from Bayefsky and Freifeld. The only other alternative, he said, given that the Minister had intervened in the matter, was for Watson and others on Council to resign in protest. But they rejected that idea; the effect of their doing so was too unpredictable. Reluctantly, they agreed to accept the Minister's proposal, including the reinstatement of Bayefsky and Freifeld. Meanwhile, Davis's staff continued to tell the media that the Minister hadn't taken sides; he had simply met with the various parties.

Council accepted Watson's — i.e. Davis's — recommendation. The Minutes stated that Council hoped that Bayefsky and Freifeld would "recognize their ... responsibilities in carrying out their duties in full co-operation with the present administration and staff and under the present regulations." But the words were hollow. Everyone knew that the two instructors had won. Council established an *ad hoc* committee, representing all constituencies in the College, to deal with curriculum problems. This was the committee Watson had kept promising. An election was held and the members of the committee were announced. Two of the three faculty elected were Bayefsky and Freifeld.

III

THE STRUGGLE BETWEEN WATSON and the conservative faculty for control of the D&P curriculum now shifted to a new front — the question of who would chair the department. Carl Schaefer had been due to retire that spring, but Watson had asked him to stay on for another year. But at the April 8 meeting of Council, Watson announced that because of "the present situation in D&P," he was rescinding his recommendation. He was no longer certain he could trust Schaefer. The irony was that although Schaefer himself was a figurative artist and shared some of the old guard's concerns, he nonetheless supported the changes Watson had proposed, including the dismissal of Bayefsky and Freifeld. A few days after the Council meeting, Schaefer wrote a wistful letter to his old friend, the poet George Johnston, saying that although it was true that student unrest was occurring on campuses everywhere, "here certain staff members caused the trouble, all based on mis-information and falsehood. Now the students find themselves out on a limb and realize they suffered and were only used as a pawn. Too bad. I was in the papers twice I think & refused to talk to the press, as the Truth is never printed. It was very upsetting for all of us, and the place now is like a morgue. I feel badly about it ...."

The chess game continued. Later that month, Bayefsky sent Watson a letter stating, "We were surprised to learn ... that you are in the process of appointing a new chair for ... D&P without consulting those most closely involved in that discipline. ... We are convinced that the contemplated appointment of a man not firmly rooted in the traditions of the Department [would be a mistake] ... the new appointment must be open to

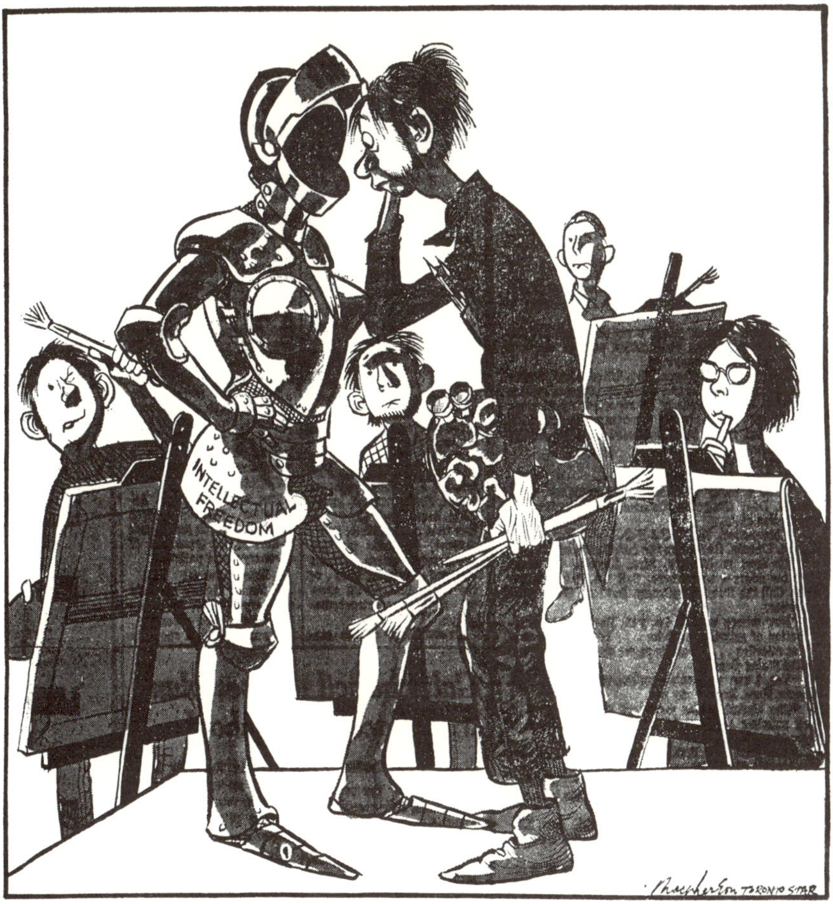

Toronto Star, March 1, 1968

all the art currents of the modern world and must possess a full understanding of the problems involved in the discipline of drawing and painting. We feel especially fortunate to have such a man in our midst … Mr. Eric Freifeld, A.R.C.A."

In his annual report to Council at the end of May, Watson was upbeat. Until the last few months, he said, "growth and change [at the College] had been successfully accomplished with a minimum of controversy in contrast with the current … unrest" on campuses everywhere. He noted with pride that OCA's facilities and enrolment had expanded during his time in office. Daytime enrolment had more than doubled since 1958 — from 479 to 1042. Evening enrolment had also doubled. Watson's report gave no hint that he had decided, or been persuaded, to step down as Principal. But at Council's annual general meeting in early June, he requested a one-year leave of absence. The request was granted. An acting principal — Gene Butt — was appointed. But as if to emphasize that Watson was no longer in charge, Council announced that it was reappointing Schaefer for another year as chair and instructor in D&P. Douglas Wright had recommended that they do so.

Savouring what he saw as a victory for The Good Guys, Bayefsky addressed a meeting of the Humanities Association that spring. He again stated that a "monolithic" establishment of art gallery owners, dealers and careerists who favoured modern art, had taken control of the Canadian art scene. "Generally speaking, the public understands instinctively that something is wrong about exhibiting a giant hamburger in an art gallery. The establishment considers the human figure and landscapes beyond the pale. Canadian work exhibited abroad is tightly controlled. Consequently, at every international exhibition we convincingly demonstrate … that nothing is happening in Canada that is not identical with the latest release from Madison Avenue." The revolution at OCA, he said, had demonstrated the problems that arise when the establishment wants to control the kind of art that graduates produce. "What we have learned," he concluded, "is that the institutions of art education must be kept independent of the establishment."

Commenting on recent happenings at the College in the July 1968 issue of *Toronto Life*, Harold Town poked fun at the students who had marched to Queen's Park: "The signs the insurgents carried," he said, "would have been rejected by striking stevedores at a local dock. This was their master stroke. Any politician in one of his right minds could instantly see that these kids were in desperate need of art training. The signs were sans serif and sans talent." At a recent party, he said, "an OCA teacher gave me an appalling account of the internecine bickering between the abstractionist teachers and the blood-and-guts German Expressionist group that has for so long dominated the painting department. … Imagine any teacher thinking there is a right and a wrong way to paint! … Hans

Hoffman, perhaps the ultimate art teacher of this century, produced simultaneously from one classroom half a dozen important figurative and abstract artists."

IV

Douglas Wright delivered his report in September 1968. In it he recommended that the OCA Act be entirely rewritten in the hope that a more representative Council would make a difference. But he had seen enough of the bitterness that existed at the College, to find it necessary to caution the OCA community that "no structure or pattern of organization will work effectively without a genuine effort on the part of all those concerned: students, academic staff, administrative staff, and ... 'lay' members' of Council." He recommended: that OCA be governed by a unicameral Council — one that took responsibility for both the academic and the administrative sides of the College. (Most universities at the time were bicameral, with a senate for academic affairs and a board of governors for financial and administrative affairs.)

Wright attributed the unrest at the College to "an obsolete and faulty pattern of ... administration. [OCA] is the only institution of its type in Ontario," he said. "The uniqueness of the College is a source both of strength and of weakness. Its relative isolation from the rest of the academic and educational world has tended to protect the College from those influences which have led to important evolutionary changes ... in other post-secondary institutions ...." He recommended: 1. That the College's CEO be designated 'President'; that he or she have one vote on a 19 member Council; that six faculty (elected) and three students (also elected) control nine seats on Council; that government appointees control another nine; 2. That OCA's program be organized into four divisions, one each for: foundation, the fine arts, the applied arts, and the evening and extension programs; 3. That the fine and applied arts divisions be subdivided into a number of departments, corresponding to the various programs of study; that there be a chair for each department, and a director for each division; that chairs and directors serve a term of three years, at the end of which they could be reappointed, but not without going through a careful review; 4. That the by-laws, minutes, policies and other decisions of Council and its committees and subcommittees be published and widely disseminated. "To the extent that students and faculty know the workings of the College's governmental system," said Wright, "they will be prepared to air their grievances through it rather than stifling them until they are vented more forcefully in other ways."

Tenure, said Wright, should be a matter "for the most careful consideration. Only a fraction of those given probationary-term appointments should expect to become tenured. Nothing is more important to the long-term development of the College than the quality of [its] teaching staff. Human nature being what it is, one of … Council's greatest challenges will be the assessment of intellectual and professional quality, especially when associated with radical personalities, against the appeal of the orthodox." He suggested that OCA become less incestuous in its hiring practices.

Bill Davis promised that the new OCA Act would be introduced in the Ontario legislature that fall. (It was introduced on December 19, 1968, but didn't pass into law until almost a year later.) Meanwhile, Council had established an Advisory Committee to assist with the transition to the new structure. It recommended the establishment of four other committees — a nominating committee, a policy committee, a budget committee, and a scholarships and awards committee. Although most members of the OCA community were hopeful, SAC's new president, Jeffery Fear, was cautious in his appraisal of the Wright report. It was based on the assumption, he said, that everyone at OCA would act in good faith. He doubted that would happen and told the *Globe* that the report might quell unrest for a time but "in two or three years we'll be back …." Fear turned out to be a prescient young man.

Chapter Three
1970

OCA's new Council met for the first time in March 1970 and for the first time, six faculty and three students sat on the College's governing body. The president and nine government appointees held the other ten seats. Among the government members sat Harold Town and the architect, Raymond Moriyami. Students had lobbied for the appointment of artists. David Owen, a lawyer, was elected chair. Almost everyone seemed hopeful. In his Toronto *Star* column, Barry Lord, a left wing art critic, congratulated OCA's students for having brought about a revolution. The only thing that concerned him was Wright's recommendation that the College be divided into faculties of fine art and applied art, "a distinction," he said, "generally considered irrelevant if not harmful in most art schools today." He favoured a more "self-directed" program in which students chose their own courses, with as much cross-fertilization as possible.

Lord quoted Monte Kwinter, a government appointee, an admirer of Buckminster Fuller. Kwinter had graduated from OCA's Industrial Design program in the mid-fifties (before the Bauhaus-trained faculty arrived). He hadn't realized, he said, how outdated the College's curriculum was until he went on to do graduate work at Syracuse University and M.I.T. OCA, he felt, suffered from "a real lack of creativity." It was "too inbred", all too frequently hiring its own graduates to teach. The New School, said Lord, which had become "a vital alternative to the provincially supported College … owes most of its success to the fact that its teachers are practising artists who exhibit original work in the city's leading galleries." It was

Art College begins a new life with students on the council

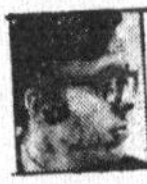

Art
Barry Lord

Don't let anyone tell you that student protests can't achieve positive or lasting results.

Two years ago the Ontario College of Art was completely disrupted by a nine-day student boycott on classes and a march on Queen's Park. The immediate cause was the firing of two sympathetic instructors (who were subsequently reinstated), but the underlying reason was general dissatisfaction with the change-resistant administration.

This week, as a direct result of those protests, the college's newly constituted governing council held its inaugural meeting, and the institution quietly started what could be a whole new life.

David S. Owen, a Toronto lawyer who is president of Merican Industries and former managing director of the Eaton Centre project, was elected chairman of the new council. But its membership is quite different from that of previous councils.

FIRST TIME

For the first time in the art school's 94-year history, students and faculty are represented on the council by voting members. Three students and six instructors make up exactly half of the 18-member board.

The other half, appointed by the government, is not exactly the crusty establishment, either. It includes well-known Toronto artist Harold Town, himself a graduate of the college, and Ray Moriyma, architect of the Ontario Science Centre.

Moriyama, for one, says he accepted the appointment only because students were represented, and because he had heard that the students suggested him.

Of course the new order is not yet democratic. Three students to represent a day-time enrollment of 1,050, and six teachers to speak for 38 full-time and 35 part-time day instructors, making up only half of the council, can hardly be called total participation.

But it is an improvement on the former 15-member board, which was completely appointed, and it does follow precisely the recommendations in the report made by Dr. Douglas T. Wright, chairman of the provincial government's Committee on University Affairs, who was appointed to investigate the college's administrative structure after the uprising of 1968.

Although Dr. Wright's report was passed as a new provincial College Act late last year, his other major organizational proposal may not be followed as closely, or may not be as popular if it is.

The act decrees a grouping of the college's present departments into divisions of fine and applied arts—a distinction generally considered irrelevant if not harmful in most art schools today.

Drawing and painting instructor Jim Tiley, one of the new faculty representatives, said that he personally favored a "self-directional network" system in which the individual makes his own course with maximum contact between departments. He said that a number of teachers opposed the divisional structure.

ALSO CONCERNED

Teachers are also concerned, Tiley said, about their lack of tenure or any other form of job security. Their faculty association submitted various briefs in the past, but the old council failed to respond. The new one, with their elected representatives on it, should be more sensitive.

An even more basic issue, and one that the council will have to begin to cope with at once, is the very question of the quality of instruction and experience in the arts that the college offers.

Toronto art teacher, camp director and former industrial designer Monte Kwinter, one of the government's appointees to the board, admitted that he came to realize the shortcomings of Ontario College of Art training after he graduated from the college in 1954 and progressed to graduate studies on scholarship at schools like Syracuse University and the Massachusetts Institute of Technology.

What was outmoded then has degenerated today into what Kwinter calls "a real lack of creativity." Most observers would agree with his comment that "the college is too inbred," hiring its own graduates as teachers to repeat the courses they studied.

In the past few years the New School of Art on Brunswick Ave., despite its lack of equipment and budget, has increasingly presented itself as a vital alternative to the provincially supported college, and many promising students have chosen it instead.

The New School is a non-profit co-operative, and owes most of its success to the fact that its teachers are practising artists who exhibit original work in the city's leading galleries.

BASIC PROBLEM

The fundamental problem the incoming councillors face at the college is to inject some New School-style dynamism into their own curriculum and its presentation. If they can't, taxpayers may begin to wonder why government dollars continue to support the college, while the New School is forced to hold art auctions to raise funds for support.

Toronto Star, March 14, 1970

essential, he said, that a revamped Council "inject some New School dynamism into their ... curriculum and its presentation. If they can't, taxpayers may begin to wonder why government dollars continue to support the College, while the New School is forced to hold art auctions to raise funds ...."

The new Council's first task was the hiring of new chairs in sculpture, printmaking and D&P. Monte Kwinter volunteered to chair the Appointments Committee and established three subcommittees — one for each position. Harold Town was appointed to the subcommittee selecting the chair for D&P. The posting described the successful candidate as "an accomplished artist with a sense of his own worth and a personal viewpoint, who is nonetheless receptive and prepared to encourage the development of other and all points of view. He should have a depth of experience and background, which will give him a sense of artistic security enabling him to work with diverse personalities. ... He must keep his department internally aware of all aspects of the art scene and should encourage on a continuing basis the utilization of visiting artists with diverse philosophies."

Later that spring, the D&P hiring subcommittee presented Council with the names of five candidates for chair — Dennis Burton, Edwy F. Cooke, John Gould, Peter Harris and Gordon Rayner. Some were abstractionists, some were figurative, but all of them, the committee felt, would be tolerant of approaches other than their own. Burton was selected and immediately turned to hiring part-time faculty for the coming academic year. Among them were David Bolduc, Tom Hodgson, Graham Coughtry, Nobuo Kubota, Ross Mendes, Gordon Rayner, Robert Markle, Dan Solomon, and Paul Young. Many of those hired had been teaching at the New School. It's not difficult to imagine the effect these appointments had on the old guard.

Burton had graduated from OCA in 1956 but was still bitter about his experience. "Instead of [a] student finding himself in school," he said, "the only choice was to find himself outside, and most never did. The maverick who challenged the curriculum ... failed, was expelled, or ignored and ridiculed." Between third and fourth year, he'd gone to study "with one of the world's great draftsmen, Rico Lebrun, in California. These 'foreign'

THE GLOBE AND MAIL, THURSDAY, DEC. 10, 1970 5

Burton, Town quit over tenure in College of Art faculty dispute

By GEORGE RUSSELL

A disagreement at the Ontario College of Art boiled over into crisis yesterday, after the resignations of fine arts department head Dennis Burton and three members of the college's governing council.

In addition, the status of another councillor and at least 20 of Mr. Burton's part-time staff at the college becomes uncertain.

The cause of the turmoil was a motion passed at a meeting of the governing council Tuesday night, which called for automatic, unconditional tenured status for all OCA faculty with six years' experience at the college.

This issue broadened yesterday, with the resignation of Mr. Burton, to include working conditions, lack of funds and a conflict of views over the entire direction of the fine arts department of the college, which includes 170 students in second, third and fourth years of painting and drawing classes.

"God help the students if that tenure decision stands," Mr. Burton said yesterday. "They're the ones who are going to get sacrificed by lousy teaching."

Two of those who resigned earlier painter Harold Town and industrial designer Monte Kwinter were provincial Government appointees to the college's 15-man council. The third, second-year OCA student Diane White, was one of three elected student representatives on the body.

All three charged faculty representatives on the council with pushing through a tenure proposal against the wishes of "every other sector of the community here" and with acting to protect vested interests in doing so.

A fourth councillor, architect Raymond Moriyama, has said he will also resign, if the automatic tenure proposal is not withdrawn pending a review.

Advising everyone connected with the dispute to "cool it,' Mr. Moriyama said the council decision was "not tolerable," particularly before the appointment of a new president at OCA.

Resigning yesterday, Mr. Burton said the dispute had to do with ... procedures ... ulty, and "continuing conflict between some of the faculty and those interested in painting post-1917."

"The tenure people are so insecure. I don't want to be a civil servant, they appear to want to be. I was trying to open up the painting department here, which was as closed as an ingrown toenail."

Administration officials at the college yesterday confirmed Mr. Burton's resignation, but refused all further comment until today.

Last night, however, Mr. Burton said he had received the support of at least 20 part-time instructors he had brought into the college, and expected they would follow his lead in resigning. If so, work in the department would come to a standstill, nine days before the scheduled end of the first semester at OCA.

"The term would have normally ended on Friday, but last week I got the agreement of the acting president to cancel exams so the kids could have more time to work."

A founder of Toronto's New School of Art, Mr. Burton exhibits regularly with the Isaacs Gallery.

He was chosen over 64 other applicants for the fine arts post and began the year by bringing in a number of professional artists as part-time and guest instructors as part of the normal program in the department.

"In the time I was there, 25 people transferred from other departments to mine. I must have spent $500 of my own money for books for the kids, and demonstration equipment." They didn't even have a ladder for students painting murals to stand on, he said.

"There is so little room in there we have kids painting in the hallways and the stairwells. I've been trying to change things around here, but I can't see it happening if people who are opposed to my point of view have tenure for seven years."

Mr. Burton stressed that he had received "great" co-operation from the acting president, Mr. Butt, and from the college's business manager.

But a further reason behind his resignation, he said, was a report that the governing council would not back a proposal that the painting and drawing classes move out of the college into rented quarters with more room.

The affair has already provoked some bitterness among councillors who resigned Tuesday night: "I could no longer sit on a council where the smell of fear was so thick you could cut it with a knife," said Mr. Town, who had favored postponement of the tenure question until the appointment of a president.

"I will never go back into the building. I can no longer tolerate the resistance of the faculty association to an investigation of the competence of the college's staff."

Although plans were not final, Mr. Burton expected to return to the college today to address the students—and he indicated that if the situation changed significantly he would perhaps return to his post. Mr. Town was also invited to the meeting, but said he would send a written statement instead.

Mr. Burton was the subject of an article in The Globe Magazine last week. It has apparently sparked ill-will among faculty and administration at OCA by speculating that the artist was bringing changes to the institution.

Mr. Butt would not comment yesterday on Mr. Burton's resignation because The Globe and Mail had published, he said, "several irresponsible articles" on the school.

The college's Student Administrative Council also withheld comment until today.

ideas affected my ... work in [fourth] year. OCA instructors refused to mark [it]; only two endorsed my explorations — Jock Macdonald and Fred Hagan. ... I stayed on because I was president of the student council and I figured I might as well get my AOCA, which by then meant nothing."

At Council's July meeting, David Owen announced that Sydney Watson had decided to retire, following his year's leave of absence. Monte Kwinter would chair a search for OCA's first President. Gene Butt would continue as Acting President for a second year. The posting read in part: "The President [will] serve as the chief planning officer of the institution, and as such has a special obligation for innovation and initiative. To the degree to which a President can envision new horizons for the institution, and can persuade others to see them and to work toward them would likely constitute the chief measure of his administration."

But before the search could begin, the College erupted again. Harry Arthurs, a government appointee to Council and himself a tenured law professor at York University, was asked to study the question of tenure at the College. He was effectively lobbied by the conservative forces in D&P. They'd succeeded in getting rid of Watson but were now saddled with Dennis Burton as chair. He and they weren't getting along. If they could get tenure before a new president was appointed, their jobs would be safe. In early December 1970, Arthurs presented a report entitled 'Proposed Principles Governing Tenure at the Ontario College of Art.' Item 14A stated: "All members of the full-time faculty who have been continuously employed for a period of six years or more as of September 1, 1970, shall receive tenured appointments." At its December 8 meeting, Council approved the document by a vote of 8-7. In favour were Arthurs, Gene Butt, and the six faculty on Council. The opposition came from the student and government members. The chair, David Owen, seemed oblivious to how contentious the issue was; he could have chosen to table the motion to allow time for wider debate.

Immediately following the meeting, Harold Town announced that he was resigning from Council. No one should be guaranteed a job at an art college, he said. Monte Kwinter, Ray Moriyama and Diane White, a student member of Council, said they too would resign if the tenure decision wasn't reversed. Dennis Burton announced that he was resigning as Chair.

"God help the students if that tenure decision stands. They're the ones who are going to get sacrificed by lousy teaching." In his fury, he made public a letter he'd written a month earlier, but hadn't sent, firing eleven members of the old guard. He spoke bitterly of the "continuing conflict between some … faculty and those interested in painting post-1917. The tenure people are so insecure. I don't want to be a civil servant [which] they appear to want to be. I was trying to open up the painting department here, which was as closed as an ingrown toenail." Paul Young, one of the new instructors in D&P, said Burton couldn't be replaced. "He has lit a fire in this school that no other department chairman ever has lit, and that fire is still going. If you want to put it out, get rid of him."

At its next meeting, on December 14, Council reversed its decision on tenure, also by a vote of 8-7. David Owen read aloud Burton's letter of resignation, followed by a second letter from Burton, seeking reinstatement. Council referred the matter to the Academic Relations Committee, chaired by Harry Arthurs. Burton was reinstated but not before he was rapped on the knuckles for making public his unsent letter. The letter, said the Academic Relations Committee, "demonstrated very bad judgement and callousness regarding the human impact on those affected by it." The Committee reminded Burton that "[d]ecisions as to staffing [must] be preceded by consultation with the Administration and … approved by Council." The statement concluded, "There is and always will be room in the Ontario College of Art for many points of view about art and art education. The College will neither tolerate interference with innovations because of vested interests nor accept the purge of individuals because they hold a minority point of view at any give time."

Town, however, had had it with the College. "I could no longer sit on a Council where the smell of fear was so thick you could cut it with a knife. … I can no longer tolerate the resistance of the faculty association to an investigation of the competence of the College's [faculty]." He vowed never to set foot in the building again. "Reflecting on his resignation some years later, Town wrote: "Over the years … I have been approached by art students complaining about the College and especially … the teachers who expressed violent opposition to abstract … art. Jock Macdonald, during meetings of Painters Eleven, often told of notifications of avant-garde exhibitions being torn from the bulletin board and described at length the ideological schisms that divided the staff. Because of this I said yes when asked … to sit on the Governing Council. … Though the College has many good people and some excellent teachers it also has a hard boil-like core of reactionaries, who over the last 20 years managed by admirable cunning to survive all attempts to get rid of them. Watching them … hastily try for tenure before a new principal was appointed, caused me to resign. … I should have known better [than to sit on Council]. It is much more important to save something like Toronto's old city hall or fight a highway than attempt to help art students who will in the end cut the mustard alone, unaided by anything other than what is in their guts."

While the tenure debate was going on, the *Globe Magazine* published an article by Barry Hale, a Toronto art critic, who described the excitement that had been generated in D&P by Burton and the new teachers. The greatest problem he and his colleagues faced, said Burton, was finding enough time to work with students one on one, in order to help them develop "their own curiosity and learning processes." Under Burton, everything in D&P was open to question. The new faculty, for example, particularly those who'd come from the New School, wrestled with the question of grading. As Arthur Handy, put it, "How do you grade them? … some of the best and most valuable sessions we've had are talking, fighting, and so on. … I took a bunch of them to the David Mirvish Gallery and we were there for hours talking about the art, what they thought about it and why. How do you grade that? That whole problem of grades is a great example of how the whole administrative function strongly influences the learning process."

Jim Tiley, an abstractionist, had originally been hired by Sydney Watson in London, England in 1961 to teach in D&P, but immediately found himself at odds with his colleagues. He moved to teaching painting to advertising students and drawing to foundation students. Tiley responded to Barrie Hale's article in a letter to the *Globe*, pointing out that Hale's piece was "neither as generous nor as impartial as it could have been toward the small handful of talented and deeply committed young painting students who, with the encouragement and assistance of some equally committed teaching faculty, have for several years … produced some very fine work in the face of bitter acrimony from reactionary attitudes around them. I'm sure that Mr. Hale has no intention of misleading his readers into assuming that efforts to introduce radical contemporary attitudes to OCA have only just begun nor, I imagine, will Dennis Burton be reluctant to share some of the kudos for what has already been achieved."

Chapter Four
1971

BY EARLY 1971, the list of candidates for president had been reduced to three names, including Alfred Pinsky, a professor of Fine Art at Sir George Williams University in Montreal, and Roy Ascott, a British artist and teacher. The committee chose Pinsky, although Kwinter and Owen, as chair of Council, favoured Ascott. Pinsky turned the job down. It was rumoured that Owen and Kwinter had scared him off by telling him that difficult decisions faced him, including the firing of faculty in D&P. Pinsky denied the rumour. In any case, Roy Ascott was offered the job, and accepted it.

Ascott had graduated in Fine Art from Dunelm in 1959, had taught at several British art schools, including the Slade, and had been a member of Britain's National Advisory Council on Art Education. Ascott had had several one-man shows and had published in academic journals. He was 37. His contract with the College stated that "always subject to the overriding authority of … Council" Ascott was responsible for "the establishment and declaration of the future aims and goals of the College." And again "subject always to the prior approval of Council" he was responsible for "the creation and elimination of divisions and departments, the appointment and removal of the heads of all divisions of departments, administrative officers, teaching staff and such other officers and employees as he deems necessary or expedient for the purposes of the College." Ascott's lawyer attempted to persuade Council to change the above wording, giving Ascott more power. He was unsuccessful.

In an article in the *Toronto Telegram* announcing Ascott's appointment,

John Fraser put the College's unhealthy state in perspective. "University fine arts departments, like the one at York, as well as the various colleges of applied arts, vie with one another on territory that was until recently, the sole preserve of OCA," he wrote. At the same time, the College itself had been "going through a period of inner turmoil, dissension and re-evaluation ... when it should have been closing ranks and looking to the future." He quoted from a recent publication by Ascott: "Fine Art teaching in its present form is bankrupt and in Design there is little more than narrow vocational processing — it trains for tasks and roles which are obsolescent," said Ascott. "As such, these pursuits are ... socially irresponsible. It is time we faced our responsibility as artists, and in consort with scientists, attempted to formulate new human values, an ethical code which would be meaningful and relevant to our evolving culture." If members of Council didn't know Ascott's philosophy of art and design education, they should have known. Ascott made no secret of his views.

Shortly after his appointment was announced, Ascott and David Owen nominated Monte Kwinter to be the College's vice-president. In a column in the *Telegram*, Douglas Fisher reported the rumour that Kwinter was being hired as part of a you-hire-me-I'll-hire-you deal. Owen and Ascott denied the rumour. They'd picked Kwinter because he was the best of 30 candidates, they said. Despite the suggestion of impropriety, when Kwinter's name was put before Council, no one questioned his appointment. Council wasn't asked to approve either a job description for Kwinter or his salary. Owen and Ascott had decided that his salary would be $27,000. Ascott's contract called for a salary of $30,000 in the first three years of his five-year contract and $35,000 in the final two. His $30,000 would be worth approximately $140,000 today.

Ascott officially took up his duties on July 1. Between July 1 and the beginning of the school year there was much to be done. New teachers had to be hired. Returning teachers had to be given their assignments. Ascott's philosophy and curriculum needed to be fleshed out and explained. He somehow expected that in two months he could transform OCA from what it had been to what he wanted it to be.

I was one of a number of non-artists Ascott hired that summer; he wanted the students to be in regular contact with "non-visually oriented" faculty, in my case, someone with a background in literature and the media. My interview with Ascott probably lasted no more than five minutes but I liked the long-haired, chain-smoking man across the desk from me and the confidence and energy he exuded. We discussed utopian novels — Ascott, too, was fond of Edward Bellamy's *Looking Backward*. And he too was interested in alternative forms of education. Later that day I was called and told that I'd been hired; I'd be teaching second year students, two days a week, at a salary of $4300. I arrived at OCA ignorant of its history and its politics. I knew no one currently at the College and only one person who had studied there. I wasn't aware that the editor at *Saturday Night*, Robert Fulford, for whom I'd begun doing some freelance writing, had recently been appointed as a government member on Council.

I had just published an article in the August 1971 issue of *Saturday Night,* entitled "The Case Against 'Education'." The piece was subtitled "If Schools Were Really Liberating, Would Government Support Them?" Toronto's garbagemen and teachers had been threatening to go on strike. Both strikes were averted. My argument was that if the teachers had gone on strike, "if the schools had been closed and had remained closed, it's likely that no great harm would have been done. Learning in Toronto would not have ground to a halt; many [students] would have continued learning, perhaps at an accelerated pace, in all the incidental and accidental ways in which they now learn just about everything anyway — from friends, enemies, relatives, television, films, books, and so on. If the garbagemen had gone on strike, however, Toronto would really have been faced with a serious problem. There are no alternatives to garbage removal. There *are* alternatives to school, most of them probably better than school."

On August 3, I attended an orientation meeting at OCA for all second year faculty. Ascott spoke at length about his program and did so with considerable energy and charisma. (The word 'charisma' had recently entered the Canadian lexicon because of Pierre Trudeau.) I didn't understand much of what Ascott was saying but I assumed that was my fault. The world of art colleges was new to me. A couple of weeks later I received a seven inch 33⅓ vinyl record in the mail, entitled *Aug. 3*. Ascott's talk had been taped; he'd been so pleased with it that he'd turned portions of the talk into a record, which was distributed to all second year students and

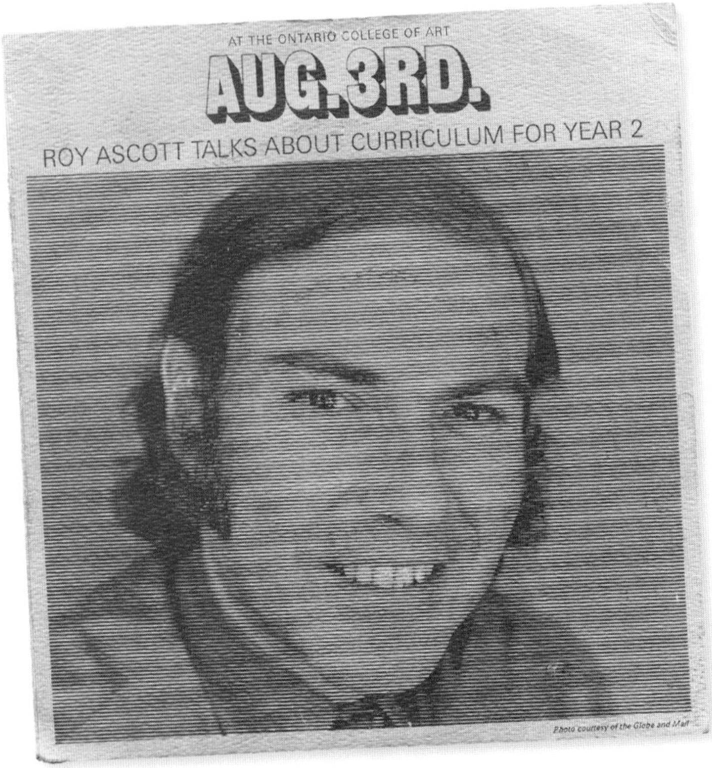

faculty. On the front cover was a picture of a smiling Roy Ascott; on the back a description of the second year program: "The year is divided into two semesters. The first is devoted to expressing a hyper-awareness of the question 'What is man?'"

I listened to the record carefully and although I was still puzzled, what he was saying made more sense to me. "The overall philosophy of the College," said Ascott, "is that we are not simply throwing out, like some sort of sausage machine, students who will simply satisfy the immediate needs of business and industry, but we are bringing students into the world who can create alternatives not just to existing jobs, but alternatives on all levels: alternative images, alternative forms, alternative structures, alternative systems … even alternative relationships between human beings." Ascott proposed to turn OCA into the world's first "visual university," a place where teachers from many disciplines rubbed shoulders and where students explored themselves and the world in whatever ways they wanted. It would be a place where learning to think came before learning technique. It sounded good.

Faculty were asked to say something about themselves for a collection of brief bios to be distributed to the students. Mine read: "Morris Wolfe (b. 1938): have been filing clerk, elementary school teacher, catalogue compiler, opportunity day boy, secondary school teacher, beer deliverer, box breaker, private tutor, oil can crimper, private school teacher, produce man, freight car unloader, university teacher, straw puller, boys' worker, editor, blueprint reader, hot dog seller, associate examiner, camp director. Currently: book reviewer, essayist, part-time teacher; interested in literature, politics, social criticism, film; married, three children; introvert, skeptic, socialist, finger nail biter, print addict, collector of old records, etc."

II

Ascott chose to conduct himself from the outset as if OCA had been handed to him to do with as he wished. He knew major changes needed to be made and so did Council. Why else would they have hired him? Without consulting either Council or most of those affected, Ascott announced that he was abolishing departments and formal classes. His OCA would be a 'free' school, a place where students reached out for what they needed to learn. The College's primary responsibility, as he saw it, was to provide as broad a range of human and physical resources as possible for the students to draw on.

Before classes had even begun, he was in trouble. Joan Burt, the president of OCAFA, presented a formal complaint to Ascott and to Charles Hanly, executive vice president of the Ontario Confederation of University Faculty Associations (OCUFA). The complaint centred on Ascott's failure to seek the prior approval of Council and its committees for the decisions he was taking. In his hurry to hire new faculty, he failed to reappoint 27 faculty from the previous year to whom OCA was contractually obligated. They'd had no word from the administration and when they called to ask what their assignments for the coming academic year were, they were told they had none. Understandably aggrieved — they assumed they'd been fired —

they complained to OCAFA, which in turn complained to OCUFA. The provincial body sent Council a telegram: "The OCUFA executive is gravely concerned at the apparent administrative breakdown in the Ontario College of Arts [sic] as represented to us by its faculty association. A case has been made to us that statutory regulations and proper academic and administrative procedure have been neglected in the governance of the College." The newly formed Academic Relations, Policy and Planning Committee (ARPP), chaired by Robert Fulford, investigated the specific portion of the complaint presented by OCAFA. The 27 faculty were reinstated; those who had accepted jobs elsewhere were given severance. Council, however, did nothing about OCUFA's more general concern about "administrative breakdown" at the College.

By the first day of classes, the College had already loosely divided into pro- and anti-Ascott factions. His supporters, for the most part, consisted of idealists and romantics. They believed, with Emmanuel Kant (whom they quoted) that "youth should be educated not for their present condition but for the possibly improved future state of the human race." Those who opposed Ascott, many of them conservative, had less faith in the perfectibility of humankind; they believed in structured and traditional approaches to art and design education. The difference was between those who regarded students as candles to be lit, and those who saw them as vessels to be filled.

During Ascott's first weeks and months, the government members on Council seemed bored, as if having hired a President freed them from responsibility for what was happening. The student and faculty members on Council were confused — and silent. Everyone on Council knew, or ought to have known, what the OCA Act required of them and of the new President. Ascott assumed that was how Council functioned, as a kind of advisory body. No one was telling him otherwise. An astute politician might have gained control of Council by winning over at least the government members at the start of what was clearly going to be a difficult year. An astute politician might have published a regular newsletter or held faculty meetings to explain and discuss what was happening at the College. Unfortunately, Ascott shared the contempt many artists have for politics, which they see as antithetical to what art is about.

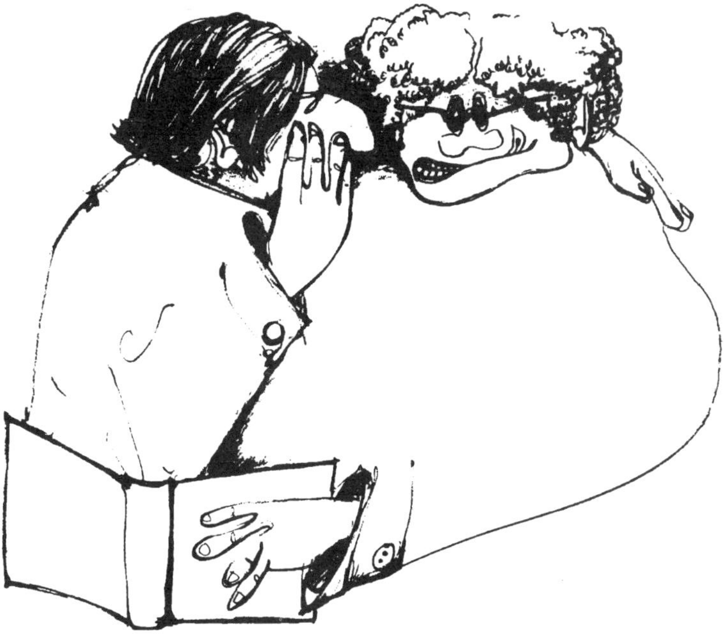

The College loosely split into pro- and anti-Ascott factions, whispering and conspiring.

Some teachers, myself included, found Ascott's program unclear and inconsistent. In theory OCA was a remarkably open institution; in practice it wasn't. (As some wag once put it, "In theory, practice and theory are the same; in practice they're not.") Aspects of the program in Ascott's 'free' school were extremely rigid. All second year students and faculty, for instance, regardless of background or inclination, were required to spend the first few weeks of the academic year discussing the question, "What is man?" That would then be followed by group projects. But it was all too amorphous. By the second week, students had begun voting with their feet. David Hall-Humpherson, the co-ordinator of the program, sent them a letter on September 24, saying, "You can not participate or collaborate effectively if you withdraw … from the community. … we need you here."

Although the program clearly wasn't working, we were told to carry on. Attendance continued to drop. One of my second year students, Max Allen, asked the question, "What is Man?" of a number of people, including a wino in Grange Park, and the then mayor of Toronto, William Dennison.

The wino commented, "Man's a fuckin' bastard … like a cigarette you find say fuckin' used up you know. Just like a fuckin' dog, say, no fuckin' place to piss, say. … you fuckin' asking me? I'll tell you … howzat?" The mayor replied, "… man must do a lot of thinking in ah respect to ah the ah population of human beings on this earth.")

In early October, Joanna van Essen, a fourth year student and a member of Council, resigned from the governing body. "Council meetings," she wrote, "consist of performances. No important matters are discussed fully. … It is now the first week of October, the students are confused and fourth year classes are non-existent. The administration seems to be so excited … but too many steps have been taken without [studying] each step. The result is confusion in many important areas." The faculty association again complained to Council and to OCUFA. Without reference to Council, OCAFA said, duly constituted committees had been abolished or ignored; heads of divisions and departments as well as teaching staff had been appointed or removed; divisions and departments had been abolished; and a new curriculum structure had been established. Although the grievances of the 27 faculty had by now been dealt with, they were in "themselves the results of inadequate administrative practices and inadequate procedures … which, we believe, have not been corrected …." At the end of October, Council still hadn't formally responded to OCAFA's concerns.

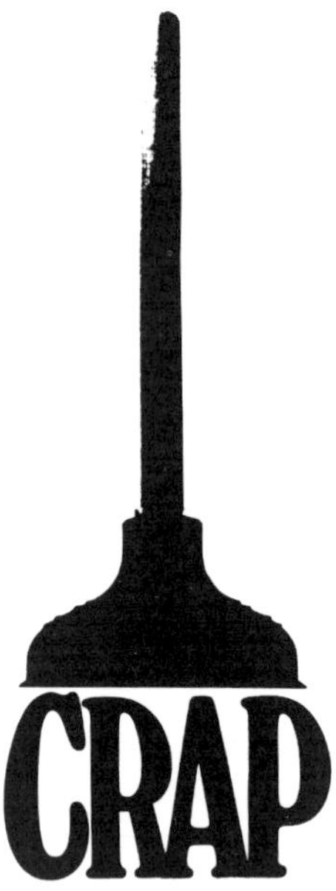

In the absence of either an administration or a student paper, three students and I began publishing a little mimeographed paper called *crap*. (Hemingway says somewhere that a good writer has a "built-in shockproof crap detector.") We would try to report as fairly as we could on what was happening at the College. The first issue appeared in October. In it I wrote, "There exists at the present time, so far as I know, no public forum at the College for a continuing discussion of the radical experiment in education we are involved in. Perhaps this magazine can serve as such a forum." I went on to say, "… I've taught in almost every kind of school in Ontario and at every … level from grade one to fourth year university. OCA is the most open school I've taught in; there's no other school in which I've felt more 'free.' What we're attempting at OCA is the most exciting experiment in post-secondary education that I know of. … Nonetheless, the openness at OCA feels too precarious, as if it exists by decree of a benevolent dictator (and is subject to his repeal), rather than as an agreed on and accepted right. … It seems inconsistent for an institution to describe itself as open … and yet to require students (all those in second year, say) to participate in a uniform program."

Ascott seemed more concerned with the historical importance of what he was doing than with sorting out the details of his program. Various speeches and meetings at OCA were audiotaped or videotaped, the idea being that when the College became famous as the world's first 'visual university,' as famous, say, as the Bauhaus, people would be able to see and hear how it was in the beginning. In our first issue of *crap*, we published a review of Ascott's record. "*Aug. 3rd*," wrote Max Allen, "proves to be an interesting if not exciting first release for Roy Ascott. He leans heavily toward the lyrics rather than the melody, making him more of a poet than a composer. Comparisons can be drawn between his seemingly disjointed ramblings and earlier works by Bob Dylan, and perhaps Leonard Cohen. … The record … may increase his small fanatical following or perhaps wipe it out completely." Ascott wasn't amused.

A number of colleagues, including John Chandler, an art critic, and one of Ascott's co-ordinators, agreed that the program didn't read well on paper. Yes, the program was ambiguous, they said, but that wasn't important. What was important was Ascott himself and the creative energy he'd brought to the College. There was no doubt that many of the best students at OCA were thriving because of the energy — and the critical toughness — Ascott and the new faculty brought to critiques of their work. Compared with Ascott's program, said David Craven, a painting student, the former program was "totally mindless." Royden Rabinowitch, a sculptor, said the best work at OCA was better than the best at the prestigious School of Visual Arts in New York, where he was also teaching.

Ascott, however, was continuing to demonstrate that he lacked the political, administrative and diplomatic skills that would have been essential to making his radical vision of OCA work. What if you're a student and don't know what to reach out for in a 'free' school or how to reach out? What if you want to take or teach classes? Shouldn't you be free to do that? Chris Symeonides, for example, had come to OCA to study advertising. That's why his parents in Greece had paid for him to come. When he'd finished first year, he assumed that beginning in September 1971 he'd be in the advertising program. No one told him otherwise until after he'd registered for second year. Even then, he did what Ascott wanted him to do — he reached out. He found a number of students who, like himself, wanted an advertising class, and a couple of instructors who were willing to teach it. But he made the mistake of asking Ascott's permission for the class to begin. Permission was denied. Advertising had no place in the kind of art and design college Ascott wanted to create.

Leonard Oesterle, a sculptor, was one of the teachers Ascott wasn't going to rehire despite the College's contractual obligation to him. When he was reinstated by Council, he put up signs saying he was going to teach sculpture *classes* — an act at OCA that seemed on a par with Martin Luther's tacking his 95 theses to the cathedral door. Oesterle used copies of well-known works in his teaching. As a symbolic gesture, Andreas Bartels, a sculptor and an Ascott supporter, smashed some of them, proclaiming, "No creative ability is developed through copying." (Many of the casts had been purchased in the mid-nineteenth century by Egerton Ryerson, the founder of public education in Ontario.) Ascott, who had earlier ordered the copies removed from the sculpture studios, agreed. "The use of copies," he said, "can be considered a form of brainwashing." There followed what Ascott assumed history would describe as The Great Sculpture Debate. Traditionalists and experimentalists gathered in the auditorium for a three-hour meeting to debate not only the propriety and implications of Bartels' act, but the question of what sculpture in the 1970s was about. The discussion was recorded on videotape. Ascott said he wanted OCA to become "the crucible of new developments in sculpture." The smashing of the plaster casts made all the papers. In a letter to the editor of the *Sun,* a reader commented, "I have visited the sculpture studios at the Ontario College of Art and came to admire the magnificent British Museum casts that have been so wantonly destroyed. … I strongly object to valuable public property being destroyed. When will Mr. Ascott … turn his attention to the books in the OCA library?"

Helen Gregor had spent a number of years building up OCA's textile department, of which she was head. She was excitable and took great pride in her students and what she and they had accomplished. Not only did Ascott abolish her department, but he said weaving didn't belong in an art college. It's just a craft. (He had similar feelings about ceramics.) Ascott's actions and comments made Gregor apoplectic. As she subsequently told Council, "Was that really necessary or wise? I ask you, was one man just arrived from abroad, the right person to make these decisions, without even the courtesy of consulting those who were affected?"

A confrontation between Royden Rabinowitch and Don Wallace, the former head of the ceramics department and an instructor strongly opposed to Ascott's program, brought things to a head. Rabinowitch, who said he wanted more critical interaction between faculty, visited Wallace's ceramics studios in what he described as "a spirit of co-operation." Wallace reported that Rabinowitch had shouted that all the work in the studio was crap and that Wallace shouldn't be at OCA. Wallace's attorneys asked Rabinowitch to desist from such conduct and threatened legal steps. Rabinowitch replied in a letter which said, "You are I trust aware that every artist must expect criticism, both from the public and from fellow artists. … Anyone who confuses argument with slander, or criticism with a damaged reputation, has I suggest serious problems of self identity and artistic security." In defence of Rabinowitch, Ascott told a committee of Council that he believed the question was one of academic freedom. Wallace's supporters replied that Ascott didn't know the difference between academic freedom and intimidation.

Wallace was so angry that he spent part of his Christmas holidays in England, checking up on Ascott. He found three people who had negative things to say about him, recorded their comments, and on his return, circulated them. The comments were subsequently turned over to OCUFA. Meanwhile, back home, the increasingly besieged Ascott opened his Christmas card from Bill Davis, who was now premier. The card had been designed by Aba Bayefsky.

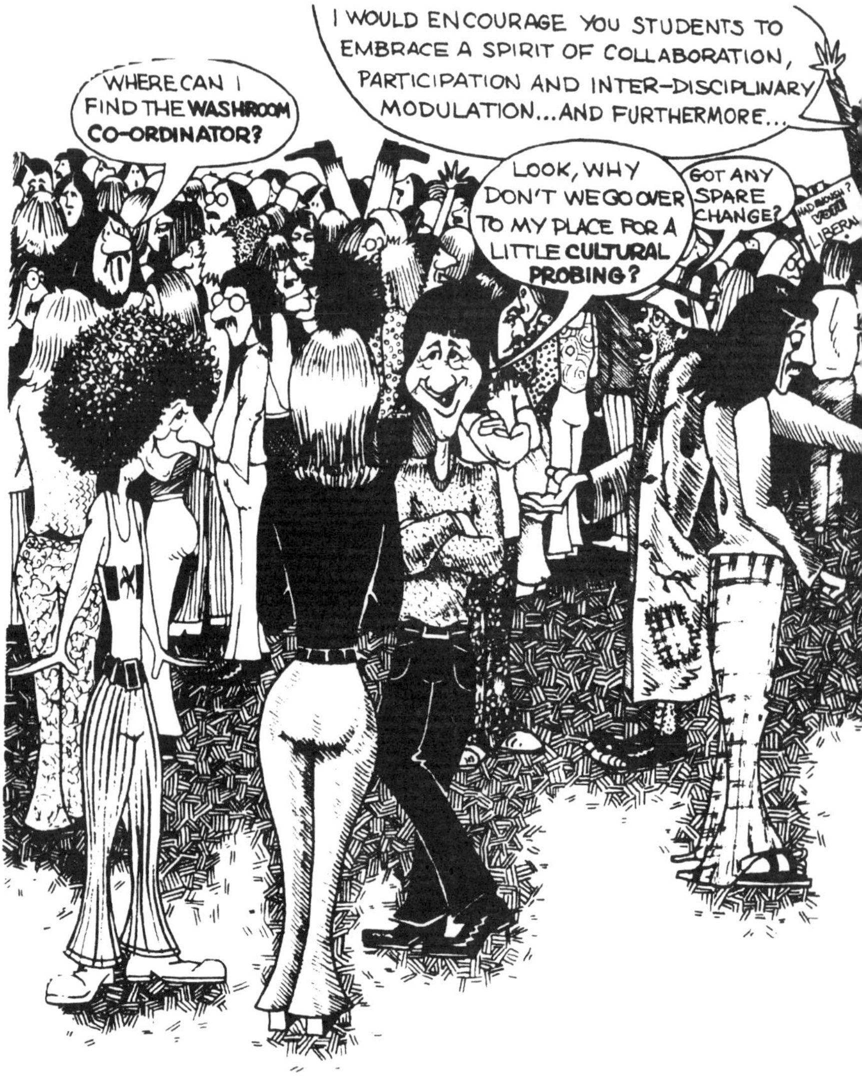

III

By mid-November, the battle lines were clearly drawn. The Great Sculpture Debate had taken place. A letter written by faculty member Eric Freifeld and signed by eleven others, including Aba Bayefsky, Helen Gregor and Leonard Oesterle, was sent to Douglas Wright of the Department of

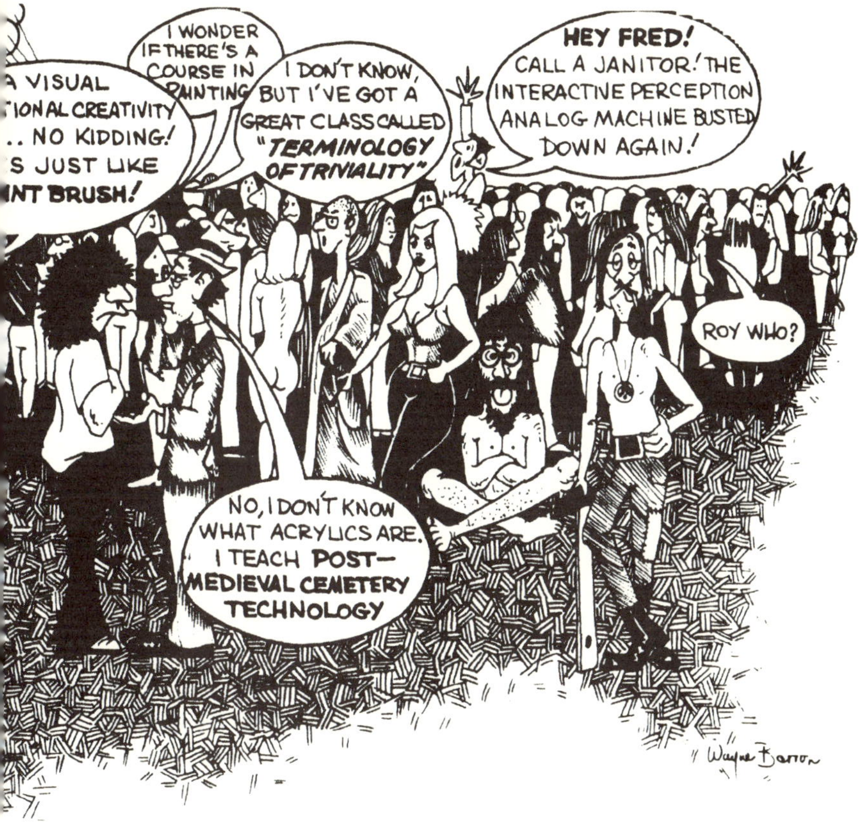

University Affairs. It criticized Council and Ascott for failing to observe due process, although they themselves had failed to do so in not taking their complaint first to Council. There was a request by the Faculty Association that OCUFA launch an investigation into the administration at the College. There was a petition signed by 345 students asking for "optional classes in the instruction of various media and techniques." Although Ascott's initial response to the petition was hostile, as it tended to be to criticism of any kind, a Skill Bank was established in January, making available the kind of instruction the petition had asked for. The Skill Bank listed faculty who had particular skills — in airbrushing or welding or whatever — and when and where they would be available to offer instruction.

It wasn't clear whether Ascott was asking for or getting advice, but if he was, he was getting bad advice. There are things he seems neither to have known nor to have had the sense to ask about. Despite the wording of his contract, he didn't understand the role of Council. (Nor, it seems, did Council itself.) It wasn't until November that Ascott understood what OCAFA was. He'd assumed it was a group of artists and designers interested in discussing art and design education and couldn't understand why its members kept behaving like a union. And he seemed to assume that due process had been invented by his enemies at OCA to keep him from implementing his ideas.

At the November 25 Council meeting, Percy Smith, VP academic at the University of Guelph and a new government member, pointed out that according to the OCA Act, it was Council's responsibility to "make by-laws and regulations for the conduct of its affairs." Where were the by-laws, he asked? Well, there were none. Council immediately formed a committee to produce a set of by-laws; Percy Smith was named chair. (One of the only matters of concern to Ascott at the meeting was the appropriateness of continuing to use the trillium as OCA's emblem.) The day after the Council meeting, the Minister of University Affairs, John White, met the nine government appointed members of Council and told them they were serving the taxpayers of Ontario poorly; they didn't seem to know or understand what was happening at the College. In the absence of proper procedures at OCA, his office was being bombarded with complaints from parents and students. His little lecture had little effect. If anything, he succeeded in getting the government members' backs up.

On December 7, at a meeting of the Academic Relations Committee, Ascott complained that he'd been called "less than honest" in a school publication. Nancy Poole, a government member, told him he needed to develop a thicker skin; he'd be called a lot worse things yet. She asked what the publication was. Ascott replied that it was *crap*. Poole wondered whether members of Council could have copies. I briefly abandoned my reportorial duties and went to get some, which Monte Kwinter then distributed. It pleases any editor, of course, to see people reading his publication. I was especially proud to see all the members of the Academic Relations Committee with *crap* in their hands.

Chapter Five
1972

THE ONLY JOURNALIST seriously attempting to make sense of what was happening at the College was John Fraser at the *Globe and Mail*. In an article in early 1972, he wrote that "the most vigorous debate on art education ever heard in Canada" was currently taking place at OCA. In an interview, Ascott had told him, "We are living in a world where nothing is inevitable or absolute anymore. … We are trying to do a lot of things at OCA right. … The most important is to equip kids with the ability to adapt and be happy in a world of accelerated change where all values are in flux. Look at … design. If we turned out kids who specialized in only one area of design, they would end up the victims of economic vagaries. … the specialist is doomed. … We want to turn OCA into a visual university that will foster creativity and criticism, that will produce adaptable graduates for whom the future holds no fear." (Many students carried around copies of *Future Shock*, during the year. It wasn't clear whether they viewed it as a sacred text or as an amulet, to keep the future at bay.)

Joan Burt told Fraser: "The new curriculum is based on just one man's concept of education and his prediction on how the future will work out. … Some of the worst mistakes would never have happened if this College had been functioning legally according to our Act." Robert Fulford told Fraser that he supported the new curriculum. The old OCA, he said, was "a marginal institution that meant nothing to the art community as a whole." Council, he said, "has got to work harder and take more authority. A visual university is a goal that must be reached, otherwise I don't see much future for OCA."

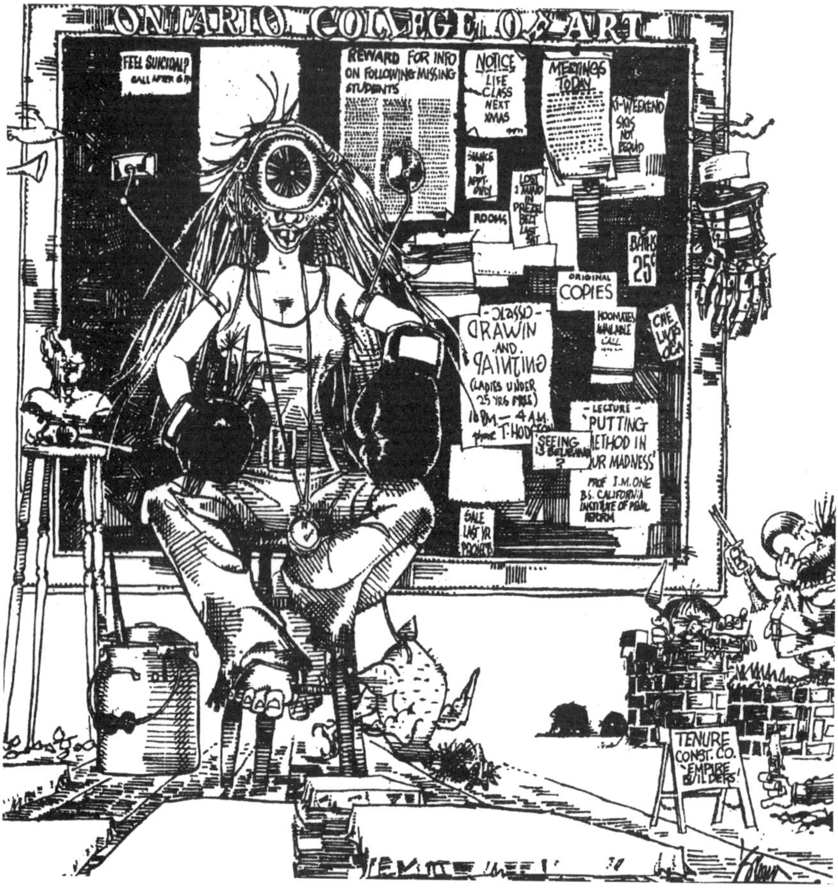

Huntley Brown, Toronto Star, March 14, 1970

It wasn't until late February that OCUFA and Council agreed to terms of reference for a three person Committee of Investigation "into the adequacy and effectiveness of the curriculum planning and academic governance processes in the Ontario College of Art." Council had been astonishingly slow responding to OCUFA's request — months went by — and even then agreed to the inquiry reluctantly. Council would "make available to the committee of OCUFA all documents available to it and … this is the extent of our co-operation at this time …." The committee, chaired by C.B. Macpherson, a respected political economist, was to investigate: a) all relevant aspects of academic governance; b) any specific or individual problem that might shed light on the general problem of academic governance; and c) the budgeting of the College. Finally, it was to formulate recommendations. The investigation didn't actually begin until March, eight months after OCUFA's original telegram to Council expressing concern about an "administrative breakdown" at OCA.

One of the more colourful faculty Ascott had hired was Frank Ogden, a "futurist." In his bio, he described himself as an "LSD therapist." Ogden hated the word 'teacher'; he was a "catalectic provocateur." You can't teach anybody anything, he said. "You just have to set up an environmental climate. Then, if something turns them on, they learn." He took students chicken plucking and to visit the morgue. One of his projects was "a 24 hour non-stop high intensity course." Students taking the course explored the AGO blindfolded; lunched on tiger meat; sat in on a Hare Krishna ritual; and watched the sun come up from the top of the TD Centre. Graduates of the course were awarded diplomas, printed on brown paper bags. They carry "as much value as any university degree," Ogden said. What the world really needed, he suggested, was more illogical thinking. "Logic only extends the known; it never creates the new. … illogic creates the new." Ogden, a tireless self-promoter, was a media darling.

At its March 7 meeting, Council announced that all faculty would be reappointed for the 1972-3 academic year. Given everything that was happening at OCA, it would have been impossible to conduct a proper review of the faculty and the curriculum. By now the rift between pro- and anti-Ascott faculty had become so wide that members of the pro-Ascott faction, led by Frank Ogden, announced they were withdrawing from OCAFA and forming their own association — the Positive Faculty Association. Implicit, of course, was that the faculty who remained in OCAFA, were all opposed to Ascott. I formed my own association — the Skeptical Faculty Association. It had a membership of one.

There were 60 full-time teachers at OCA eligible to vote for faculty on Council. More than 40 part-time teachers, including myself, didn't have the vote. The 60 full-timers split roughly 35-25 against Ascott. The 40 part-timers split about 50-50. But the six faculty on Council all opposed Ascott. When they'd run for Council, they behaved like real politicians; they phoned and button-holed colleagues, urging them to vote. The pro-Ascott forces, like Ascott himself, didn't take College politics seriously and weren't organized.

In late March, Kay Kritzwiser, the *Globe*'s art critic, reviewed the College's annual exhibition of student work and was impressed. She delighted in the children's shovels and pails outside each exhibit room. "A great idea," said Kritzwiser, "a cocky answer to the inference made of late in the press that OCA students were like a lot of kids playing in a sandbox." She found the work of senior students particularly impressive. "The maturity and professional scope was on a record level," she wrote. She particularly singled out the light lab exhibit, a project Ascott had encouraged. "This one vital recognition of the field of electronic art alone helps to counteract OCA's unfortunate image, fostered by all that silly business of students eating rattlesnakes and passing out garbage bag diplomas."

II

COUNCIL DIDN'T MEET again until April 19. Meetings scheduled before then had been cancelled for lack of a quorum among government members. Then, at the April 19 meeting, the roof fell in. After some mundane housekeeping matters had been dealt with, David Berg, a student member of Council, asked the Chair, David Owen, if student and faculty members of Council could present a report. Since the report dealt with personalities, they requested that Council move *in camera*. The vote for moving behind doors, was 10 in favour, four against, including Ascott. (Four government members were absent; one seat on Council was vacant.) The room was cleared and a motion was presented: "[T]hat Roy Ascott be suspended as President of OCA for a period of 60 days pending an investigation into his function as chief executive officer of the College; the investigation to be conducted by the Council of the College." The vote was nine in favour, four opposed, with one abstention. All six faculty members, two of the three students, and Fulford made up the nine votes. It was then moved "[T]hat in the absence of a recommendation, the one year contract of the Vice President not be renewed." The vote was 10 in favour, three opposed, with one abstention. A motion was then put that "Because this is probably the last meeting [of] the academic year ... an election be held for Chairman of Council now." Nancy Poole was nominated and there being no further nominations, she was declared the new Chair. (It's surprising in retrospect that one or more of the government members didn't leave the room, thus breaking quorum.)

When faculty and students waiting outside the meeting room heard what had happened, they rushed in, shouting abuse. Some of them had been drinking, a point made much of by the old guard. Throughout the year lifestyle had become a minor but real issue. Dress and cleanliness were part of it — sex and drugs more so. Anti-Ascott faculty said that some of his supporters were sleeping with students and that others did drugs with them. During the shouting that followed Ascott's suspension, one faculty member on Council was taunted with the suggestion that he'd probably voted as he had because he hadn't been laid since he was 21.

Royden Rabinowitch was outraged. "Roy Ascott," he announced, "is the most extraordinary man I've ever met. Here's a man who doesn't believe in training people, *training* people. He believes in looking at a person and considering deeply that person. He's the most extraordinary man I have ever met and I have met extraordinary people. I'm an extraordinary person myself. They fear Ascott because he's absolutely moral. Christ was strung up. So was Socrates. And they're trying to do the same to Ascott. These people can't be destroyed. The moral forces of the world will triumph. Hitler didn't last." Frank Ogden declared, "I think it was a criminal conspiracy and it should be treated as such; ... if they're guilty

Apparent coup by faculty

Suspend art college president

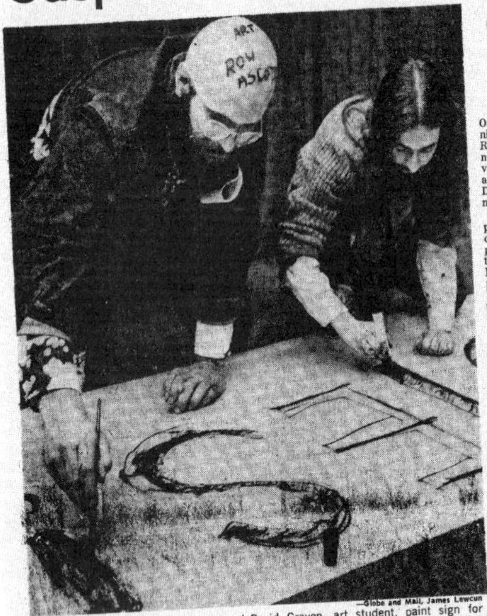

—Globe and Mail, James Lewcun

James O'Donnell, video instructor, and David Craven, art student, paint sign for demonstration today in support of Roy Ascott, president of Ontario College of Art.

Council takes action against two others

By MICHAEL VALPY

The governing council of the Ontario Council of Art last night suspended its president Roy Ascott for 60 days, voted not to renew the contract of vice-president Monte Kwinter and replaced businessman David Owen as council chairman.

The council's 9-4 vote, apparently a well-organized coup by faculty members opposed to Mr. Ascott's administration and radical curriculum innovations, ordered the president's suspension so that his "function as chief executive 'officer of OCA" could be examined.

The motions dealing with Mr. Kwinter and Mr. Owen followed in swift succession. There was no hint of what the anti-Ascott faction—the six faculty and two of three student members of council—had in mind until they suddenly introduced a motion to close the meeting.

Mr. Kwinter, an industrial designer given a one-year contract as vice-president last summer by Mr. Ascott, was asked to leave the room along with about 20 instructors calling themselves the Positive Faculty who had turned up to defend Mr. Ascott's program.

After the suspension motion was passed, the 37-year-old president walked out of the meeting, stunned by the decision.

Then Mr. Owen walked out after the motion to elect a new chairman. He was followed by Paul Moore, the only student council member to vote against the suspension, and provincial Government-appointed council member Douglas Trowell, president of radio CKEY, who announced he would resign.

Attending the meeting were four of the nine Government appointees—the bare minimum for a quorum—and the full complement of faculty and student representatives. Saturday Night editor Robert Fulford was the only Government appointee voting in favor of suspension.

Mr. Owen, who was replaced as chairman by art gallery owner Nancy Poole—the only council member nominated—said testily later that his removal was "just part of the whole thing. That's all I'm going to say. I'll say a lot in a week, or maybe a day, from now."

Mr. Kwinter said he was not too sure what had happened. "I just don't know that much," he said. Mr. Ascott, a British painter and art educator who was appointed last June, left the college without talking to reporters.

Meanwhile, students and faculty members supporting the president planned a demonstration for today—the same day that press and leading art gallery owners from Eastern Canada have been invited to OCA for the annual scholarship awards exhibitions of student art.

At the core of the trouble is the philosophy Mr. Ascott brought with him to OCA that swept the college suddenly into a new, foundation-jarring era of computer-age art forms, the language of McLuhan and cybernetics, in fact the remolding of the whole institution to fit the views of Mr. Ascott and the people he brought with him.

It was to be, as the new president described it, "an organic art community developing creative individuals with no preconceptions about what art is or isn't other than that it is a visible means of humanizing society."

The faculty members and students who supported him spoke of the new excitement of freedom in the college—the oldest institution of its kind in Canada and for years condemned by leading figures in the art world as more of a glorified trade school than a true college of art.

But on the obverse side of the coin, Mr. Ascott's critics are convinced that the college has been turned into a shambles.

They point to the 20 per cent student dropout since Mr. Ascott took over. They talk of the illegal firings of faculty members who did not fit in with Mr. Ascott's vision.

A faculty group led by architect Joan Burt, president of the faculty association, has complained both to former Minister of University Affairs John White and the Ontario Confederation of University Faculty Associations which

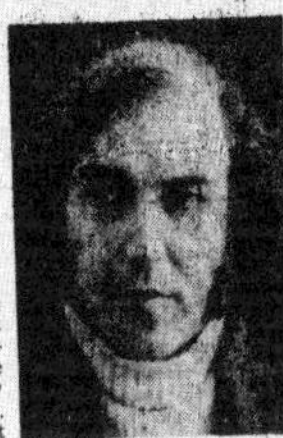

Roy Ascott

has just completed an investigation of OCA and will be reporting next week.

Burton Raffel, the OCA's senior tutor—a position created by Mr. Ascott when he brought Mr. Raffel to the college—resigned last week, leaving behind him a document that calls the Ascott program "basically fraudulent, although not intentionally".

Mr. Fulford said in an interview he had become convinced the college was in a disgraceful state.

"A great many students do not attend. Hundreds of students have been alienated by the new program along with many instructors both new and old."

Both Mr. Fulford and Miss Burt said the decision to replace Mr. Owen as chairman was made because it was time to have a new chairman. Mr. Owen had occupied the post for two years.

Globe and Mail, April 20, 1972

they should go to jail." John Chandler said Ascott had been "hired as a person with vision not as a person with administration experience." David Craven commented sadly, "If Roy Ascott leaves, this school will die."

The next day, furious faculty and students met to discuss strategy. Two hundred students signed a petition demanding that the two students on Council who had voted to suspend Ascott, resign their seats. The student body had been apathetic when the original election had taken place. Sixteen members of the Positive Faculty Association, issued a writ, declaring Council's proceedings invalid on the grounds that Council was illegally constituted. The election of faculty, they claimed, had been improperly conducted; among other things, ballot boxes had been left unattended. One Positive Faculty member, Ray Lichtman, a teacher of philosophy and science fiction, didn't sign the writ but said, "I'm very sorry this had to happen. Now … Council has polarized things. Now I can't really say, 'Well there are a lot of things wrong with Ascott's program.' And there are. But I can't say that any more. I've got to say I'm with Roy 100 per cent now. They've made me do that. I think it's very, very destructive."

OCAFA's executive met later that day, surrounded by Ascott supporters. They passed motions censuring the faculty on Council for suspending Ascott without having consulted them, and asking that the suspension be lifted. Two members of the OCAFA executive later reversed their votes, saying they'd voted as they had because they were intimidated. One of the Positive Faculty members who suggested that the writ be dropped so the two sides could begin talking again was told he'd be beaten up if he didn't keep quiet. "It would be a major mistake," said Fulford, "to think that this is a case of the reactionary forces versus the progressive forces. I think it's a case of the possibility of maladministration versus the possibility of good administration."

The *Toronto Star* reported that applications for the next academic year at the College had declined by over 50 per cent. Students thinking of enrolling in 1972–3 were being sent OCA's new calendar — a set of tarot cards. A self-congratulatory *Sun* editorial stated that what had happened at the College "was a flop, catering to a minority. [This paper] first brought the controversy to public attention … the smashing of plaster copies of famous works; the unrest among some students and faculty; the listed 'artistic' qualifications of teachers, such as LSD therapist; … oil can crimper …."

KENNETH BAGNELL

A spanking at OCA

The discord now shaking the Ontario College of Art should surprise nobody and for at least three reasons. First, the college president, along with a number of faculty, has tried to change the place not merely around the edges, but at the very centre. Second, the college has been bruised internally in recent years, a bad strike, a divided faculty and much insecurity. Third, and most important of all, we are dealing with artists, the most creative of the creative people, and to expect of them an administration that is calm and ordered is asking for the moon. As a result of all this the college president, Roy Ascott, in the job only 10 months, stands suspended by his governing council, apparently for being high-handed, abolishing exams, scrapping courses and firing faculty. Such accusations may be exaggerated, but there is a lot of evidence that Mr. Ascott was fast with the broom; and this in an institution of deep passion and division. So a commission of Ontario educators has put him over the knee, spanking him for trying to change the college with an approach that is contrary to the college act and to the way things are done in the university community of Canada. Mr. Ascott, it might be noted, is not a local boy. And yet OCA knew, when they appointed Roy Ascott for a five year term, they were appointing a president who vowed to change the college, to make it a highly creative, experimental place. He stood for a new kind of OCA and he said so when he was approached last summer. It must have been apparent to the OCA people who selected him that they were not acquiring a president who would go about putting out old fires, but lighting new ones.

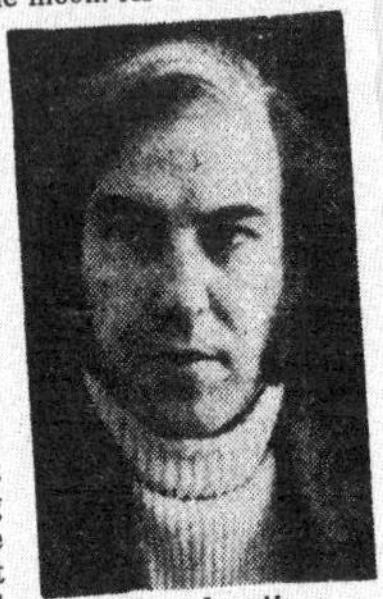

Roy Ascott

In view of all this, it seems a little unfortunate that less than a year afterward the governing council, at least the majority, should decide that Mr. Ascott isn't performing the way they'd like. They claim many students are unhappy and that large numbers are not bothering to show up for classes. Maybe; maybe not.

But this is hindsight and does not meet the present circumstances of the college. No matter what the cause, the problems are real and the commission is right in placing much of the fault not on personal attitude, but on procedures that stem from an outmoded system of internal government. It is a system which apparently almost bypasses the faculty and is as appropriate in today's academic community as a lawn mower in a hayfield.

Probably Roy Ascott is not an administrator and has no inclination or perhaps aptitude to become one. Few artists, musicians and writers do. But the larger question is whether he ought to be one. It would be helpful; but is it necessary? Must OCA be run along lines such as the large academic institutions so that its president is in reality a politician?

If it must be this way, then art colleges will never settle down into ordered institutions, unless of course they are to forsake experimentation and return to classical forms and more structured purposes. Perhaps they should. But that is clearly not the mood of the moment among artists. And so, having called a man of a deeply innovative style, it seems only fair that the college, in some way, adapt to him, and not just he to it.

Globe and Mail, April 20, 1972

It's not clear when Council members first saw the OCUFA Report, which was dated April 18 — the day before Ascott was suspended — but wasn't made public until several days later. The report stated that before Council had put an adequate academic structure in place at OCA, "a new president was appointed, who had staggeringly different ideas, from any that had prevailed before, as to what a college of art should be." The OCUFA report made a number of detailed suggestions on: how to prepare a budget; the importance of circulating agendas and background papers prior to meetings; and the creation of an adequate committee structure. Council, the report continued, had been "seriously negligent in performing the duties given it by the Act. … The first meeting of the new Council was held on March 11, 1970. In the two years since then … Council has taken no effective steps to establish the substructure recommended by the Wright Report nor to establish policies on appointment and tenure. Instead, it has, in dereliction of its duties under the Act, left many crucial decisions to be made by the president without any discussion by Council or any consultation with such academic boards or committees as were deemed essential by the Wright Report."

A *Globe* editorial commented, "The Ontario College of Art has lately been engaging in one of its periodic attempts at self-immolation, and in the fitful light of what seems to be going on there, it may very well succeed this time. Certainly there is no more than a month or two left to restore some semblance of order, if the fall term is not to open on a spectacle of empty student places and idle teachers. … [Mr. Ascott] appears to suffer from a singular inability to work with people who disagree with him. … His educational approach is aimed at encouraging excellence in the exceptional student, but, as the distinguished British art historian and critic, John Russell, has pointed out, '… the exceptional student has a way of getting through in any case. Systems are made for the unexceptional student, and their object is that the unexceptional student should be a more valuable human being for his years at art school — and have some chance of earning his living in a way that is congenial to him.' The College has to be concerned with the needs of all its students."

On April 25, Council announced it would establish a three-person inquiry of its own. Ascott and the Council would each appoint a member;

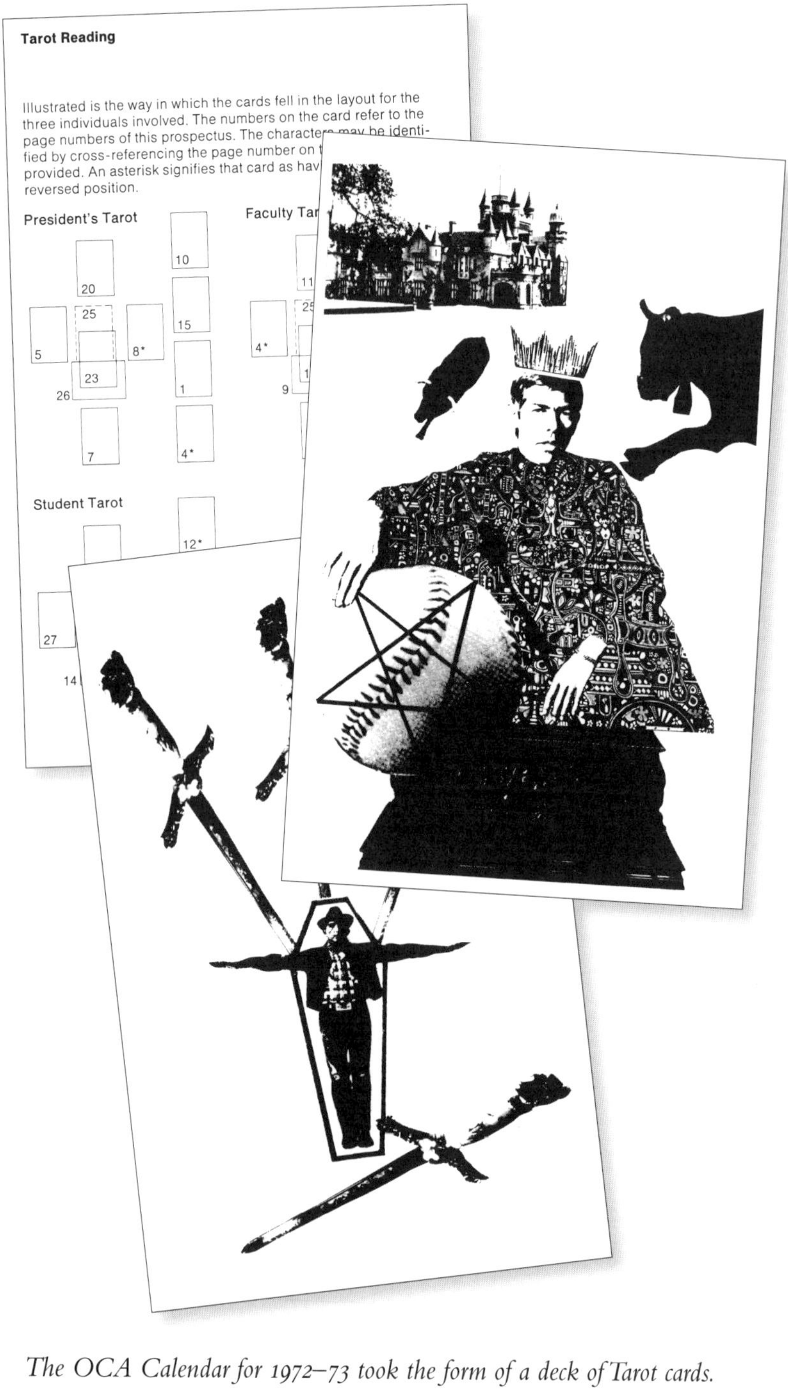

The OCA Calendar for 1972–73 took the form of a deck of Tarot cards.

those two would then choose a third person as chair. Council had by now hired a lawyer to sit in on its meetings. Monte Kwinter had a lawyer. Ascott, his lawyer at his side, told a press conference that he was going to ignore the suspension and wouldn't co-operate with the inquiry. "I warned … Council when I started that the first year might appear chaotic." The Positive Faculty had a lawyer. Their writ, seeking an injunction against Council, was proceeding. (It was later denied.) "At the latest count," Alexander Ross wrote in the *Star*, "there are now five sets of lawyers involved in this dispute, and none of them comes cheap."

In the absence of a president, Council appointed a five member executive committee to run the College, consisting of Nancy Poole, the chair of Council; Joan Burt and Bob Mitchell, faculty on Council and co-ordinators in Ascott's program; David Berg, a student; and Robert Fulford. Ascott continued to occupy his office following the suspension and to attend Council meetings, even though he wasn't allowed to speak or vote. But when he arrived at the College on May 5, he discovered that he'd been locked out of his office. On May 18, Council, having failed to establish a three-person inquiry, decided to proceed with one, Harry Arthurs, who was no longer a member of Council. He was to examine "in general the discharge of Mr. Ascott's functions as President of OCA, and in particular all aspects of his relationship as chief executive officer with the administrative officers and staff, the academic officers, the faculty and the faculty association, in regard to the obligations imposed upon him by the Ontario College of Art Act and his contract." Arthurs was to begin on May 23 and to turn in his report on June 2.

Some of the most sensible comments about what had taken place came from students. The following letter, for instance, had appeared in the *Toronto Star* in mid-May: "I have just completed my third year at the Ontario College of Art. Up until now, like the majority of students, I have kept quiet in the turmoil surrounding the college, mainly to keep my sanity. The general idea behind the new program is admirable. … The main problem … was not in the program itself, but rather in the way it was thrust upon all four years of the college. People need time to adapt to a new idea. The general lack of organization … resulted in quite a few students suffering disorientation, apathy, confusion and the hostile feeling that someone was experimenting with their futures, and not too successfully. No one likes to be a guinea pig. … if the program were introduced gradually, a year at a time, instead of in one staggering jolt, the Ontario College of Art would resume its role of providing competent artist-designers to a world that will need all the help it can get."

At the end of May, Ascott published an article in *Art Magazine*, entitled "Art as an Alternative to Education, or, The Demise of the Jam Factory." Art education, he said, "in its present form is synonymous with intellectual torpor and its controlling image is that of the jam factory. … a place or situation in which old values are conserved or pickled, and that may, through this process, produce something that has a rather sweet taste but which is seen in fact to be rather cloying after a period of time. There is a concept of art … which says that art is a regurgitation of past values, art is a pickling process … a matter of conservation of what has been the case. But artists refute this. Creativity looks for the new. To be an artist is to stalk the unknown, to find what could be the case rather than to examine merely what has been the case. As artists we celebrate the future. We are turned on to the future. We create the future."

III

Harry Arthurs delivered his report on June 2. "I have no mandate," he said, "to consider the educational quality of the program instituted under Mr. Ascott's presidency. It may be that this program constitutes a brilliant break-through in art education, as his supporters contend. It may be that the program represents an educational disaster, as his detractors contend." Echoing the OCUFA Report, he said that Council "was hardly vigilant in the defence of its constitutional and contractual rights." Traumatic changes had been allowed to take place without full preparation either by the administration, or the students who were to be its beneficiaries." Ascott's program and administrative structure were "never reviewed in detail or approved by Council." The program had been worked out by Ascott and a small committee during the summer of 1971 but wasn't actually presented to Council until November. Implementation of the program became the task of the President's Advisory Committee (PAC) [comprising all the co-ordinators], whose existence Council only became aware of in February 1972. "It is quite clear that ... PAC ... virtually supplanted the consultative and decision-making procedures required by the Act, and effectively obviated the necessity for Council itself to embark upon a detailed development of the academic philosophy and program of the school. This was unconstitutional." Arthurs continued: "The temptation for Mr. Ascott to cut corners in matters such as consultation and prior approval must have been very great. It was not resisted." Ascott, said Arthurs, "was at some pains to point out to me that he made no claims of experience in administration, and did not consider that he was hired as such."

Prior to a Council meeting on June 16, George Kerr, the Minister of Colleges and Universities, asked if he might address Council. Sounding like a lawyer for the defence, he implored Council to "keep the interests of the institution at heart in deciding Ascott's future." He hoped Ascott had a "future role" at OCA although he realized that Ascott "might require ... administrative help." The future of the College was in jeopardy, he said. Kerr was reiterating comments he'd made earlier in the legislature, in responding to a question from the leader of the NDP: "... my initial reaction to the problem ... was that this man needs a chance. You can't prove anything in one year. I think the fact that first-year students think he's great is characteristic of the type of curriculum that he is trying to invoke there. I suppose where you have a second-, third- or fourth-year student who is used to another type of curriculum and philosophy, he is bound to react differently than a first-year student."

Just days before Council decided what to do about Ascott, Vince Kelly, Council's lawyer, checked his credentials and references, something Council hadn't done when he was hired. The Ipswich School of Art, where Ascott said he'd been Head of Fine Art from 1964-1967, informed Kelly that he'd held no such post. He'd been a Senior Lecturer responsible *to* the Head of Fine Art. In 1966 he'd been told he was 'redundant' but was given an extension until he found another appointment. The director of the Polytechnic in Wolverhampton, where he went next, confirmed that Ascott had taught there but said he'd had no administrative responsibilities. (Ascott's résumé stated otherwise.) The director went on to say that "As a teacher [Ascott] was brilliant and highly articulate. Only in the matter of his relationships with colleagues was there any reservation about his contribution to the faculty; it was thought that he could have adopted, with profit, a more flexible attitude."

At the June 26 meeting of Council, the chair asked Ascott and his lawyer whether they preferred that the new information — the matter of his credentials — be discussed in public or *in camera*. They chose the latter. It was moved by Roy McMurtry, a new government member on Council, "that Mr. Ascott does have a future role at the College." The motion was defeated 9-8, the eight consisting of seven government members and one student. Fulford moved that Council request Ascott's resignation. The vote was 11-1 in favour, with three abstentions. Council moved back into public session and announced that "A resolution was passed today … requesting that Mr. Roy Ascott submit his resignation as President of the College. Mr. Ascott then tendered his resignation which was accepted and a mutually satisfactory settlement was made with respect to the termination of Mr. Ascott's contract." (He was given $45,000 — a year and a half's salary.) Following his resignation, two more government members of Council resigned in protest; one of them was Ray Moriyama.

In the June 1972 issue of *Toronto Life*, I published an article entitled "Ascott in Wonderland." The article appeared three weeks before Ascott was fired. In it, I wrote that a "great many mistakes have been made by almost everyone — especially the Council that hired Ascott and then left him to fend for himself. They must have known they'd hired a man who has a talent for provoking conflict." I said I hoped his contract would be renewed, and that even just as theatre, Ascott at OCA was too good an act to break up.

I'm not sure what ultimately tipped the scales in favour of dismissal. Perhaps Ascott's fudged credentials were the final straw. The swing vote was Robert Fulford. If you're a government member on Council and take your job seriously — not many do — there's a lot of work involved, especially if you chair a major committee. (Government appointees on Council donate their time.) Fulford, perhaps the hardest working government member on Council, realized probably more than anyone how hard he and his colleagues would have to work if Council were to rein Ascott in. The idea of finding an able administrator must have seemed awfully tempting.

Council spent the summer of 1972 writing by-laws, struggling with the College's accumulated deficit, and conducting a search for an acting president. Somehow it seemed fitting that Clifford Pitt, a 57-year-old educational psychologist, should be hired. Pitt, who was well connected with the educational bureaucracy at Queen's Park, persuaded the Davis government to pay off the accumulated debt. The government's willingness to do so, Pitt said, was "a clear indication that [they are] willing to support us as long as we have a stable and responsible administration." If the College was to survive long term, he stated, "It is no good paying lip service to some highly desirable ideal only to find out that implementation produces the very reverse of what we most want. Our future must

be workable." Pitt was a decent, hard-working man and an able administrator. But no one would ever mistake his niceness for a vision. The OCA he took over in the summer of 1972, he later said, was "like entering a madhouse. The place was in a complete state of anarchy. It was as though the lunatics had taken over the asylum ...."

In an op-ed piece for the *Toronto Star* during the summer of 1972, Ascott wrote that he was convinced that had he remained at OCA, "the philosophy of art education which I had been hired to implement would have been heavily ... [compromised]. ... In place of the new philosophy ... [I can already see] no more than a ragbag of confused intentions, muddled thinking and a well-intentioned but foolish yearning to be all things to all men — the politician's dream. ... Our intention was to make OCA the leading centre of advanced visual education in North America. ... We thinned out the plantation of looms, intruded on the boutique and cottage industries of knitting and weaving, figurine manufacture and therapeutic potting. ... we abolished departments with their territorial rights and compartmentalized minds. ... we made room for the technologies of today. ... we encouraged video and electric media in many forms; a superb light laboratory was set up; plastics were given as much recognition as plaster had been. ... we made the first small steps toward computer-aided design and we brought in fresh minds to deal with cybernetics, philosophy, mathematics, the physical sciences, psychology, literature and music. We said to each other: 'the old ways are dead, let us invent the new'."

Chapter Six
AFTERMATH

THE CONSERVATIVE FORCES quickly took control of the College, re-established departments, and appointed themselves chairs or, in some cases, became the powers behind figurehead chairs. Bob Mitchell for example, became chair of Communication & Design, and Joan Burt of Environmental Design. Franklin Arbuckle, an illustrator, was named chair of Fine Art. (Eric Freifeld became chair not long afterward.) There were two notable exceptions. In a conciliatory gesture to Ascott's supporters, Clifford Pitt and the chairs created a small Experimental Art Department, its faculty made up of abstractionists and other avant gardists. Royden Rabinowitch was named chair, but he was even more unsuited to administrative responsibility than Ascott; he treated his job as a joke and soon left the College. The other exception was the creation, under Richard Hill, a McLuhanite, of a small Photo/Electric Arts Department, with hands-on and academic courses in photography, film, video, and computers. (I taught film history courses in Photo/Electric.) Along with Ex Arts, we were separated from the rest of the College and housed in other buildings.

In the fall of 1972, Pitt and the chairs invited the OCA community to participate in exploring alternative futures for the College. What kind of school should OCA become? Various proposals were written, brought forward and considered. One alternative — Future Zero — would have shut OCA down and had it start over. (Not a bad idea, a kind of institutional version of divorce.) Ascott's supporters proposed 'Future Zed'. "An art college," they wrote, "being a community of artists and scholars, should

As long ago as the P.A.C. meeting of Dec. 13 there had been talk of a new school. "John Chandler hinted that there were some students planning to start a new art college. This plan was presently at the conceptual stage" (from the minutes of that meeting). Starting in mid-January, a number of faculty and students met to discuss things on a more concrete level. It had been suggested by some supporters of Future Zed that the realization of that philosophical direction would have to be preceded by Future Zero, a term coined the Ellis Report referring to the possibility of closing O.C.A. Many Zeddites now felt that their best bet would be to completely abandon their attempts to get O.C.A. to adopt Future Zed, and instead start from scratch on their own. "Instead of being negative, we're doing something positive," said student Paul Casselman. On Feb. 9 the new school, called **Z**, set up a booth to talk to interested students and faculty, and to collect enough money ($1600) to rent space (8800 sq. ft.) until the end of May. On Feb. 15 about 150 people—faculty and students—marched down to the corner of Duncan and Pearl to celebrate the birthday of art and the birth of Z. Various newspapers and TV stations conducted interviews with those people sometimes regarded as the founders of Z: John Chandler, Tom Hodgson, Bob Kaiser, Dennis Pike, Paul Casselman and Barb Laffey. On March 14 the school space and the adjoining room were transformed into "Gallery Z" for a two-week show featuring the work of the new school's faculty, students and sympathizers. Available at the show is a 5-page description of Z's philosophy and aims for next year. It sounds very much like Future Zed, and includes under "curriculum" an outline for first year consisting of exactly the same subjects (in name, at least) currently being taught in first year at O.C.A. How can you get in? "A student shall be a student if any of the teachers claim him as a pupil." So far Z has lined up 20 "regular" faculty (all presently with O.C.A.) and 48 visiting lecturers (11 of whom are now with O.C.A.). 125 students have paid $15 for Z membership, good until May, but nobody can say how many will be enrolling next year, for a tuition fee roughly equivalent to that of O.C.A.

be the avant garde of postsecondary education. It should anticipate change rather than be imitative. It should be a responsible alternative to the failures of contemporary universities and colleges. … Our present schools and … students and teachers have become too goal-oriented; education has become mere job-training. … It is time we began to consider the possibility that schools are not only places where students go to 'become' but also places where students go to 'be'."

Four months later, however, in January 1973, the administration announced that the contracts of most of the faculty Ascott had hired would not be renewed. That the College had too many teachers and not enough money was undoubtedly true. But the decision about who would be let go was taken without a review of the faculty or the curriculum. Many of us concluded that the 'alternative futures' exercise had been a sham. The future had already been decided by Pitt and the chairs. Following the dismissals, a hundred students and faculty, carrying lit candles, marched from OCA to an old knitting mill on Duncan Street to establish 'Z'. They raised enough money to pay the rent until the end of the term. Faculty from York, U of T, and OCA offered to teach at Z. The school's organizers were convinced that other students from OCA would soon flock to it. It didn't happen. Within a year the school was dead.

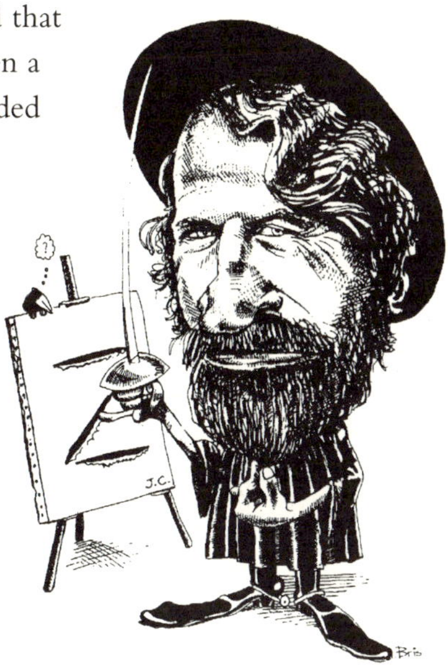

By the fall of 1973, the old guard had succeeded in putting a lid on things that, for the most part, remained in place through the rest of the 1970s and the early 1980s. Alliances between and among the conservative chairs, deft use of *Robert's Rules of Order*, and a narrow definition of what due process meant, were skillfully employed to maintain the status quo. The chairs, whose jobs and terms were never defined, and whose performance was never reviewed (contrary to the OCA Act) came to dominate all aspects of the College — OCAFA, Council, and the President. They also did all the hiring. When Paul Fleck, the President who succeeded Pitt, tried to break the chairs' hold on the College, life was made so miserable for him that he resigned and went off to run the Banff Centre.

Old problems were either ignored or swept under the carpet. OCA became probably the only art and design college on the planet with two painting and drawing departments — one in Experimental Arts and the other in Fine Arts. That there were two departments had nothing to do with the best interests of the students, of course, only with keeping warring factions apart. Because no one was prepared to knock heads, this situation was allowed to continue for almost twenty years.

The question of tenure was quietly taken off the table and replaced by an unwritten understanding that there were permanent faculty, who had *de facto* tenure, and there were part-time faculty, whose reappointment from year to year depended on remaining in the good books of the chairs who had hired them. Only egregious behaviour was sufficient for dismissing anyone with *de facto* tenure. I know of only two such cases — one for statutory rape. Merely being an incompetent teacher was never an issue.

It wasn't until the mid-1980s that the conservative hold on the College began to loosen and a shift to a more democratic OCA slowly gained momentum. Members of the old guard began to retire. Younger, more independent members of faculty, were being elected to Council. Another independent, young faculty member became President of OCAFA. A new memorandum of agreement established hiring committees and procedures. Two chairs, who had held onto their positions since 1972, were forced to leave the College during the presidency of Norman Hathaway for seriously abusing their power. A Task Force on the Status of Women was established. At the time, male faculty at OCA outnumbered female faculty by 4-1. The subsequent bitter fight for employment equity at the College during the 1989-90 academic year represented, in a sense, a final battle between the conservative and the progressive forces. The victory meant that a younger generation was taking control of the College and more importantly, its curriculum. (I published an article in the December 1990 issue of *Saturday Night* describing the struggle for equity. I've included it among the pieces in *Essays, Selected and New*, at www.morriswolfe.com)

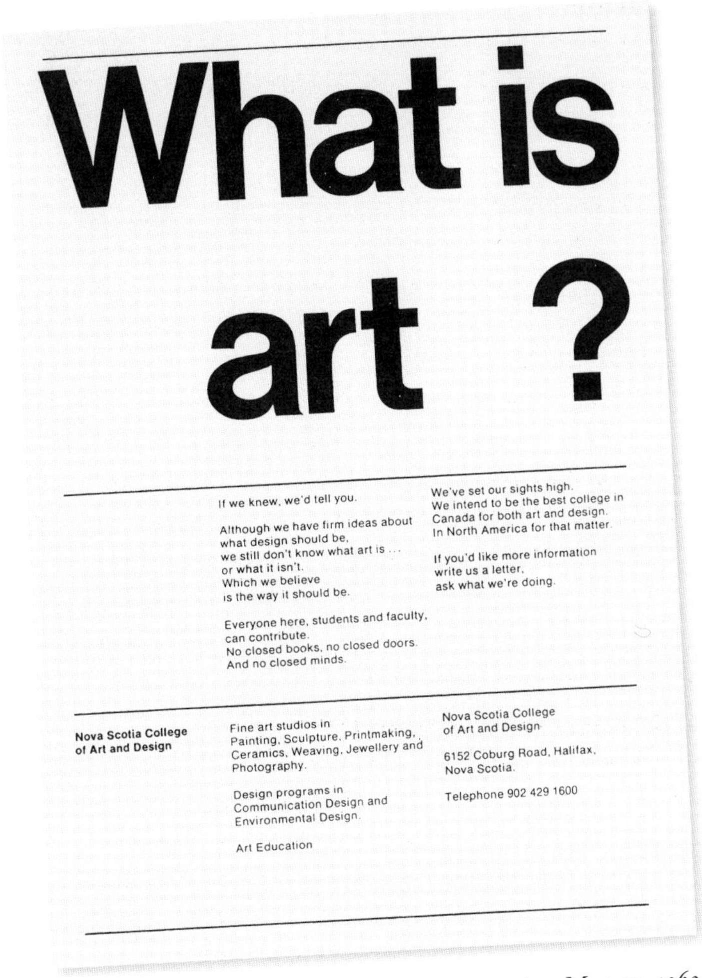

TIME Magazine, May 23, 1969

II

In the early 1960s, the Nova Scotia College of Art (NSCA) struggled with problems not unlike those at OCA. The school day still began with prayers. The approach to teaching in the fine arts was conservative and academic. Drawing from the nude was a relatively recent practice. In 1967, Gary Neill Kennedy was appointed President of NSCA at the age of 32. He'd been born in St. Catherines, Ontario, was a graduate of OCA, and had completed an MFA at Ohio University. Kennedy had only been out of graduate school for a couple of years when he was named President.

Like Ascott, Kennedy had almost no administrative experience. But he was eager to learn, shrewd politically, had a clear sense of the kind of College he wanted NSCA to become, was able to communicate his vision, and was blessed with both a dean and a Board that made up for his lack of experience. In Nova Scotia as in Ontario, the growth of postsecondary institutions was being encouraged by the provincial government. Within two years, Kennedy had succeeded in tripling the available physical space at the College; had developed a design program; had chosen not to renew the contracts of some faculty; had begun hiring leading edge artists and designers; and had obtained degree granting status for the renamed Nova Scotia School of Art and Design. NSCAD was soon being described as "the best art school in North America" (Les Levine). All that with an enrolment in 1970 of 389, up from about a 100 a decade earlier.

Nor was there ever any doubt at NSCAD that the school's primary purpose was to provide an education in the fine arts. *artscanada* devoted its fall 1968 issue to "the new education in the arts." Kennedy described NSCAD's philosophy: "In the fine arts we operate on the premise that we do not know what art is; however, we do know that the student must participate in the formation of his program if it is to be meaningful. Our obligation to the student in fine arts is to expose him to professional people and provide him with the best possible facilities and equipment." The list of visiting artists that students at NSCAD were exposed to during these years is a 'who's who' of minimalist and conceptual art.

"We recognized," Kennedy continued, "the need to bring the ideas embraced by the early years of the century from the margins into the core of the art school curriculum. We needed to acknowledge that we were the heirs to the great art of the dadas, the futurists, the surrealists, the constructivists. Pop artists, fluxus artists, happenings and performance, innovative dancers, filmmakers and musicians, were all out there. All we had to do was bring them into the institution." In a *National Post* review of a Kennedy retrospective in early 2001, John Bentley Mays quoted Derrida, who had argued that universities ought to become places where "you may search, just for the sake of searching, and try for the sake of trying. So there is a possibility of what I would call playing." The early years of Kennedy's tenure at NSCAD, Mays said, "were testaments to the power of such playing ...."

In his essay 'Self-Reliance,' Ralph Waldo Emerson defines an institution as "the lengthened shadow of one man." That's true of Kennedy's NSCAD. It was true of Watson's OCA. And although thirty years have gone by since Roy Ascott was appointed President at OCA, his shadow still haunts the place. People continue to praise or blame him for a variety of things both good and ill that in most cases have little or nothing to do with him. Still, it says something about the leadership the College has had since then that Ascott overshadows all others.

III

I've tried to tell this small part of the OCA story as fairly as I can. At the same time, I haven't disguised my own biases. I was ambivalent about Ascott. What he was attempting to do at OCA was enormously exciting. But he was also an intellectual bully; he reminded me of the Pierre Trudeau who had invoked the War Measures Act just a year earlier, saying "Just watch me" when asked how far he was prepared to go. But given what has — and hasn't — happened at OCA in the three decades since Ascott was fired, I now believe that getting rid of him was a mistake. It wouldn't have been easy to make use of his considerable strengths as visionary and teacher, while curbing his excesses. He would have needed a strong academic dean, a gifted executive vice president, and a Council prepared to work hard. Hindsight, of course, is easy. But that doesn't mean one shouldn't exercise it. What else are we to learn from if not the past? As Kierkegaard said, "Life can only be understood backwards but must be lived forwards."

Appendix One
ECHOES FROM THE PAST

TENSIONS BETWEEN those who are certain they know what art is — or isn't — and those for whom the question is open, have, of course, always existed. That's what the struggle for control of curriculum is about. The trick for an administrator at an art college is to recognize and manage those tensions.

In 1919, George A. Reid, OCA's Principal, hired Arthur Lismer to be his Vice Principal. Lismer had spent the previous three years heading up the Nova Scotia College of Art (as it was then called). As a young painter, Reid had been dismissed by members of the Canadian establishment as an 'eliminator,' a derisive term used to describe experimentalists. "Reid," said one critic, "could easily ruin Canadian art; but there's one thing, no one will ever want to buy his pictures." Before long, however, he himself had become a member of the establishment. And by 1920, when the Group of Seven mounted its first exhibition, Reid's was one of the influences the Group was reacting against.

It didn't take long for Lismer and Reid to clash. Increasingly frustrated by Reid's academic and conservative approach to the curriculum, Lismer resigned from OCA in 1927. Some of his students left the College in protest and established a school of their own, The Art Students' League, with Lismer as their teacher. Reid took a year off and then was nudged into retirement. At a dinner in his honour in 1929, Reid defended himself, "When Impressionism came in I experimented with it, and found it both, as to vision and technique, worthy of respect but only as a phase of art....Post Impressionism, Cubism, Futurism, Vorticism, Expressionism have arisen of late…as efforts to cast off the academic.…The academic was never static, although at times it may appear so.… [And] all that is named modernism is not necessarily modern, but only the old cry for something new at any cost. Abrupt attempts to change the course of human thought to attract attention causes art to fly away, leaving only folly as the residue." Lismer's name wasn't mentioned that evening, nor does it appear in the 1946 hagiography Reid authorized. Many years later, commenting on the differences between the two men, A.Y. Jackson said they typified the controversy that was then raging "between the academic painter and those who, like the members of the Group of Seven, believed that Canada could never be adequately expressed on canvas by a rigid traditional style."

Following his departure from OCA, Lismer became an internationally respected teacher. He created a Children's Art Centre at the Art Gallery of Toronto; organized a similar project in South Africa, under the auspices of the Carnegie Foundation; was a visiting professor at the teachers' college at Columbia University; directed educational activities at the National Gallery in Ottawa; and was principal at the Montreal Museum's School of Art and Design. Lismer's pedagogy derived from his belief that children were by nature original and creative and that all too often art instruction stifled them and ended up killing their natural talents.

II

JOCK MACDONALD, like Lismer, was born in the United Kingdom and trained as a designer. He came to Canada in 1926 as head of design at the Vancouver School of Decorative and Applied Arts. Frederick Varley was head of its Department of Painting, Drawing and Composition. Under Varley's influence, Macdonald began painting landscapes; by the mid-thirties he had begun exploring abstraction. Frustrated by the conservatism of VSDAA's curriculum, Varley and Macdonald left in 1933 and established their own short-lived experimental school, the British Columbia College of Arts. The Depression made the continued existence of their school too difficult.

Macdonald was hired by the Drawing and Painting Department at OCA in 1947 and between then and his death in 1960, he had an enormous influence on many of the young abstract painters who came to prominence in Toronto in the 1950s and 1960s. William Ronald, for example, had initially enrolled at OCA in 1945 and then quickly dropped out. He was "sickened", he said, by the College, filled as it was "with war veterans and debutantes, Sunday painters and dilettantes." And he was weary of the Group of Seven's influence, which he described as a "curse on the scene." He was looking for something new and found it in Macdonald, who had persuaded him to return to OCA. In 1953, Ronald, Harold Town, Jock Macdonald and other abstractionists formed Painters Eleven. They were at first ignored by the Canadian establishment but when a 1956 group show in New York was enthusiastically reviewed by Clement Greenberg, the painters quickly found support at home.

Macdonald's success made the old guard in D&P, notably Aba Bayefsky, Alan Collier and Eric Freifeld, apoplectic. Not only was the enemy in their midst, he was getting a lot of attention. Students had to be protected from his influence if at all possible. They tore down notices Macdonald put up announcing current and upcoming exhibits of abstract art. But his own students loved him and he reciprocated. He was their mentor, encouraging them, buying their work, arranging shows for them, loaning them money, constantly making them aware of recent developments in the art world. Equally important, he was a teacher who never stopped learning himself, in contrast with his figurative colleagues who seemed to him engaged in "academic sleep-walking."

In her 1965 essay on what was wrong with Canada's art schools, May Cutler argued that "[t]he most highly and frequently praised art training [in North America] is not that of any school, but of a single teacher — the artist Hans Hofmann who runs his own classes." (Macdonald spent a couple of summers in his studio.) Too bad, she said, that Macdonald hadn't been able to do the same thing in Canada.

Appendix Two
OCAD: A BRIEF CHRONOLOGY

1872 Ontario Society of Artists (OSA) founded; one of its objectives the establishment of a School of Art

1875 Ontario Department of Education gives OSA grant of $1,000 to open an art school

1876 Ontario School of Art opens in rented space at 14 King St. West

1883 School taken over by the Department of Education; moved to Normal School Building in St. James Square (current location of Ryerson Polytechnic); the school flounders

1886 OSA again takes over school; name it Toronto School of Art; location: 20 Queen St. West; the school flounders

1890 Department of Education takes over again; location: 173 King St. West; OSA tries, unsuccessfully, to establish rival school; uncertainty about what kind of school needed

1910 Toronto School of Art and Central Ontario School of Art and Design both housed in upper floors of Grange

1912 Department of Education decides one large provincial art school desirable; Ontario College of Art Act creates OCA; annual grant $3,000 and free premises in Normal School; George A. Reid appointed Principal

1919 OCA Act amended; College now governed by a Council of 23 members, none of whom are faculty or students

1919 Reid appoints Arthur Lismer his Vice-Principal

1922	New building designed by Reid opens in Grange Park; first building erected in Canada solely for purpose of art education; reflects post-WW1 cultural nationalism; Premier Drury declares, "We are building a Canadian civilization."
1924	Lismer increasingly at odds with Reid; impatient with conservatism of OCA
1927	Lismer resigns; some of his students, led by Edna Breithaupt, set up an alternative school, The Art Students' League, where he can teach; location: gatekeeper's house on Grange Road
1928	Reid is nudged into retirement; J.E.H. MacDonald named Principal
1932	MacDonald dies in office; Fred Haines named principal
1933-45	Haines arranges for OCA faculty to study with members of Bauhaus who have fled to the U.S.; courses in Material Arts begin to be taught at OCA
1945	Influx of war veterans; Design School opens on Nassau Street; more feisty students appear; William Ronald, e.g., complains that OCA "filled with...debutantes, Sunday painters and dilettantes"; dismisses influence of Group of Seven as "a curse on the scene" and quits College
1947	Jock Macdonald, a non-objective painter, begins teaching at OCA; believes growing emphasis on design is "undermining the fine arts at every turn;" meanwhile, his figurative colleagues at OCA work to undermine him
1955	Sydney Watson principal; successfully lobbies government for money to grow the College
1957	100 McCaul, first addition to OCA building in Grange Park, opens; OCA's full-time enrolment approximately 500
1962	A second addition, including a cafeteria-auditorium, opens
1965	Ontario College of Art Faculty Association is formed
1967	A third addition to 100 McCaul opens; arrangement with University of Guelph for OCA students to obtain degrees

1968 The sixties finally arrive at OCA; students strike to protest firing of two faculty members, Aba Bayefsky and Eric Freifeld; full-time enrolment approximately 1000; The Wright Report, reviewing governance at OCA, proposes a radical reorganization of the College; context in which OCA exists has changed; other post-secondary institutions offering a range of programs in art and design

1969 New OCA Act passed; for first time students (3) and faculty (6) represented on 19 member Council; Gene Butt, acting President

1971 New Council hires young artist from England, Roy Ascott, as President; Ascott assumes College has been handed to him to do with as he chooses; he abolishes departments and classes; pro- and anti-Ascott factions quickly draw battle lines

1972 Council suspends and then fires Ascott; Clifford Pitt, a psychologist, becomes President; departments and traditional curriculum quickly re-established; two important exceptions: Experimental Art and Photo-electric Arts established

1975 Paul Fleck is named President; Liberal Arts expanded

1979 Stewart Building (on College Street) acquired

1982 Clifford Pitt returns as Interim President

1983 Norman Hathaway is President

1986 New Memorandum of Agreement establishes formal hiring procedures; Committee on Status of Women at OCA created

1987 David Hall-Humpherson Acting President

1988 Tim Porteous becomes President

1989 Employment equity battle takes place; cause: male faculty outnumber female faculty 4-1

1989 OCA declares itself "insolvent"; Minister of Colleges and Universities asks Ontario Council on University Affairs (OCUA) to investigate; conclusion: OCA largely to blame for its financial problems

1991 Minister calls for external review of OCA's mission, programs and operations

1992 Task Force concludes OCA "can continue to play an important role in the university system" but the College needs help in making necessary changes; a Restructuring Team is appointed, to conclude its work in 1994-1995; during this period, Deputy Minister discusses closing OCA or folding it into another post-secondary institution, possibly Sheridan College

1995 Alan Barkley named President; three women deans appointed; College renamed OCAD; degree arrangement established through British Columbia's Open University

1997 Peter Caldwell is Acting President; negotiates acquisition of new facilities in Village by the Grange

1998 Catherine Henderson is named President

2000 Ontario government gives OCAD $24, 000,000 toward new design building; College agrees to increase full-time enrolment by 500; Ron Shuebrook named Acting President

2001 OCAD celebrates its 125th anniversary